What they are saying….

Jim Mannoia is a parent, partner, professor, prophet, pundit, physicist, philosopher, and erstwhile president and provost. All these roles permeate the range of insights exhibited in these chapel talks on the meaning of character during his decade as President of Greenville University. Though originally given during particular seasons, they remain timely. Though primarily intended for his students, they apply almost universally. Though limited by the constraints of a chapel talk, they deftly explore a range of issues we all contend with as followers of Christ. Take each one daily. And…enjoy!

Stan D. Gaede, Past President
Christian College Consortium & Westmont College

In Paradox and Virtue, my friend Jim Mannoia, drawing on scripture, his background in physics and philosophy, and the crucible of experience, tackles such diverse and important topics as suffering, character, paradox, and that most neglected of the theological virtues: hope. This is an important and timely book, leavened with both common sense and worldly wisdom.

Randall Balmer
John Phillips Professor in Religion, Dartmouth College

Jim Mannoia is an outstanding Christian philosopher whose ultimate concern for his students has always been character formation. This is a great revolution from what the academy became after the Second World War; too abstract to be a meaningful instrument for change in society. Anyone who reads this book or attended these compelling presentations at Greenville University will appreciate his focus on these concepts.

Jameson Kurasha
Professor of Philosophy and Higher Degrees Research, Zimbabwe Open University

Paradox and Virtue

Talks to My Students

V. JAMES MANNOIA JR.

WESTBOW
PRESS®
A DIVISION OF THOMAS NELSON
& ZONDERVAN

This book is a work of non-fiction. Unless otherwise noted, the author and the publisher make no explicit guarantees as to the accuracy of the information contained in this book and in some cases, names of people and places have been altered to protect their privacy.

WestBow Press books may be ordered through booksellers or by contacting:

WestBow Press
A Division of Thomas Nelson & Zondervan
1663 Liberty Drive
Bloomington, IN 47403
www.westbowpress.com
844-714-3454

ISBN: 978-1-6642-2093-5 (sc)
ISBN: 978-1-6642-2094-2 (hc)
ISBN: 978-1-6642-2092-8 (e)

Library of Congress Control Number: 2021901339

Print information available on the last page.

WestBow Press rev. date: 3/1/2021

CONTENTS

To the Greenville College students to whom these were addressed,
and Ellen my wife who loved me patiently.
They were with me then and not now...
And
To Elizabeth my wife who loves me fiercely.
She was not with me then, but is now...

FOREWORD

The "President's Course" is a highly honored tradition of Christian higher education. During Colonial times, a college identified as "Christian" was distinguished by morning chapels in which the president addressed the assembled faculty and student body. Just as chapel was defined as the "President's Course," the chief executive also carried the responsibility to serve as "First Member of the Faculty." Accordingly, the President's early morning chapel address was expected to set the text and the tone for the teaching and learning process in the classes and discussions of the academic day. Through both preaching and teaching, the President energized the mission, acknowledged the issues, confessed the dilemmas, invoked the Word of God, personalized the faith position, and called the assembled students to personal commitment.

With a sense of loss, we remember the "President's Course" primarily as an historical artifact. Christian college and university presidents still speak in chapel, sometimes in sequence, and almost always with the thought of advancing the mission and personalizing the purpose of faith based learning. Few presidents, however, adopt the chapel as their "bully pulpit" where they fulfill their primary duty to create a climate that adds meaning to the teaching of professors and enriches the learning of students.

Jim Mannoia, in *Paradox and Virtue*, brings back the value of the "President's Course" for contemporary Christian higher education. Even though the chapel addresses that he records come in the middle of the morning and at the beginning of each semester during his ten-year term as President of Greenville College, there is no question that they set the text and the tone for the campus. As I read them, I also see a pattern of presentation that serves as a model for presidents who are speaking as "First Member of the Faculty." This is an honored role that has been either lost or diminished in the expectations for presidential leadership. I plead for its recovery and offer Jim Mannoia's addresses as encouragement.

Permeating every chapel address that is included in *Paradox and Virtue* is the Mission of Greenville College. No matter what his subject, Mannoia invariably returns to the balance of Character and Service. At one time while reading, I remember chuckling as I thought about the man who loved sandwiches so much that he had one for lunch every day. A trip to the dentist upset his schedule and locked his jaw, but not his taste. He put a sandwich in a blender and sipped his lunch through a straw. For me, this bit of humor holds a compliment for Jim. By returning to Character and Service as the touchstone for every address he gave, Jim Mannoia fulfills the first priority of presidential leadership.

Close behind his emphasis on mission, Jim develops his theme of *Paradox and Virtue*. His "Introduction" is a masterful presentation drawn from his scholarship as a physicist and philosopher. With students in mind, Dr. Mannoia poses the meaning of paradox out of discoveries in physics, finds in them the tensions of philosophy, and offers the hope of resolution in virtues. With the keenest of scholarly insights, he writes:

> Virtues demand that we embrace apparent contradictions, that simple formulas are rarely enough, that living the moral life will require a crucial balancing act, an essential tension, an embracing of paradox.

But then, he challenges his readers to stretch through paradox to the highest and best of human learning:

> ... following Jesus Christ will require a paradoxical balance of passionate commitment and epistemological humility available only with intentional self-conscious effort and discipline to meet and trust the Person who is Himself Truth.

The stage is now set for adventures in paradox and discoveries in virtue.

Astute readers might ask if the theory of paradox is too advanced for the average college student. The question is fair, but the author has the answer. Jim Mannoia is a storyteller. He knows that the quickest way to spark the interest of a student mind is to suggest, "Let me tell you a story." Each chapter begins with a story from the personal history of the president. World travel is the favorite subject, but local encounters have their share of copy. In the end, you know Jim Mannoia as a man as well as you know him as President.

All these components come together in each chapter around a relevant passage of scripture that molds diverse thoughts into a meaningful whole. I am reminded of the process that my friend Bernard Ramm describes when divine revelation meets human reason. He says that there are three possible outcomes. One, when revelation and reason agree, we assert the Truth. Two, when revelation and reason are at odds, we address the error. Third, when revelation and reason are suspended in tension, we accept the imponderable for continuing research and study. Although the process is not exactly the same, I feel as if the author is taking us on the same journey when divine revelation meets human reason.

True to his heritage as the son of a strong biblical preacher and himself a lifelong student of the Word, Jim Mannoia does not leave his chapel audience suspended in tension without resolution. Rather, with the compassion of the pastoral presidency, he urges his hearers to embrace a discipline that involves risk and trust on the way through paradox to the virtues that are born of Christ alone. Needless to say, *Paradox and Virtue* deserves a visible place on the shelf of books that will shape the future of Christian higher education.

David L. McKenna
President Emeritus
    Seattle Pacific University,
    Asbury Theological Seminary,
    Spring Arbor University

PREFACE

Over the decade from 1999 until 2008, I served as President of Greenville College, now Greenville University. Located in rural Illinois about forty miles east of St. Louis, Greenville was founded in 1892 by the Free Methodist Church, a small Wesleyan denomination, born out of the antislavery movement of the 1860s. It emerged from a previous institution, Almira College, founded on the same site in 1855, a women's school. From these roots, like so many other small church related liberal arts institutions founded in that era, arose a rich heritage, over 150 years old, of educating for character. This has been my passion.

Greenville also had significance for my family. My father, V. James Mannoia, and several of his siblings graduated there in the middle of the last century. For relatively poor south side Chicago Sicilian immigrants to pursue tertiary education said a great deal about my grandmother Maria Mannoia, and about her commitment to Christian character. My sister Sharla, her husband, along with two of her children also graduated there, and continue even now to serve Greenville University. In a longstanding tradition for naming residence halls after women of character important to the college, one of the newest halls was named for my late wife, Ellen, who died from cancer during our term as President and First Lady.

When I arrived in 1999, one of my earliest efforts was to review and revise the Mission Statement. For many years it had included reference to Service. But my own philosophy of education went beyond that to include both service and character. And an earlier president had remarked that our mission would "always be to educate for character." So, during my first year we expanded our Mission and Seal to include "Education for Character and Service." The mission statement was revised to read: "*Greenville College transforms students, for lives of character and service, through a Christ centered education, in the liberating arts and sciences.*" For a decade I felt it was one of my most important tasks to articulate and promulgate this mission among faculty and staff, among donors, and perhaps most importantly among our students. At Freshmen orientation sessions both on and off campus I would divide large groups of students into four sections and have them repeat out loud *en masse*, the four phrases of that Mission statement.

In 2000, I published a book, *Christian Liberal Arts: An Education that Goes Beyond*, which lays out my philosophy of higher education along these same lines. I argue there that higher education has twin purposes, one practical or instrumental, the other personal or intrinsic.

The practical purpose is to prepare graduates for sacrificial Christian service to the world, distinctively by teaching them to think and act *integratively* in order to tackle real world problems. Contributing to this outcome are the multiple transferable skills included in any strong liberal arts curriculum (reading, writing, researching, thinking, communicating, collaborating), then broad foundational knowledge of the arts and sciences, and finally, more narrow disciplinary skills which would facilitate their securing at least the first of their likely many jobs over a working career and lifetime. In a market rapidly swinging to the vocational, we were unapologetic in claiming a solid liberal arts education was probably the *best* possible practical preparation for career, at least certainly for the long term.

But even closer to our hearts, and more at the core of what made Greenville different, was our simultaneous and even greater commitment to the personal or intrinsic value of higher education. It would not be enough to train graduates to serve. Merely training our graduates with skills could, as President Leslie Marston had said long before, produce "monsters." What was needed equally, was education for character. This educational outcome was rapidly becoming extinct in American higher education. It could only be accomplished by focused intentional attention to human development. Cognitive, moral, and spiritual development theory suggested that growth in these areas is accelerated when there is an intentional program of simultaneous and balanced *"stretching"* and *"nurturing."* Just as any wise sports coach knows that physical development requires stretching muscles even to the point of pain, so it follows that moral and spiritual development, character development, would require stretching moral and spiritual muscles. But to stretch too far causes irreparable damage. So just as a good sports coach monitors her athletes and nurtures them in a supportive community, so moral and spiritual coaches on the faculty and staff of an institution like Greenville would also monitor their students and nurture them in supportive community. This delicate balance is the genius of character development and at Greenville we set out to make that balance the "guide star" for the creation and monitoring of our curriculum and co-curriculum.

Into this environment, I felt my role as President was to model both character and service, to facilitate programs that encouraged them, and to speak to them whenever possible. I encouraged community service projects like Habitat, introduced and taught a capstone course for all seniors which tackled real world problems in cross-disciplinary teams, and spoke whenever I could on these themes.

I was normally called on to speak to the entire campus community at least twice a year at the opening convocations each semester, and sometimes at the end. Altogether, there were more than thirty talks given over the decade. From the beginning it seemed to me that somewhere on campus, someone needed to speak explicitly about what character actually looked like. To my mind, our character is the sum of our virtues. So, it seemed to me that unpacking individual virtues would be a small contribution I could make. Each time I spoke, I tried to identify one or two character virtues and then illustrate them from events in my personal life and in the current events of that day.

It is these convocation talks, these efforts of a college President to speak to his students, that you find in what follows. I have attempted to cull the better ones, without any certainty I have succeeded. They can be read in any order, with or without the overarching framework of "Paradox and Virtue" laid out in the Introduction. But I beg the reader to recall these were delivered orally, over the course of ten years, themes and stories repeated again and again to a constantly changing group of students, illustrated with events then current but some now forgotten. I have wrestled with these factors as I considered this publication. The repetition seems largely unavoidable as I felt obliged to refresh the mission to different generations. And it was tempting here to try to replace the oral delivery style with a more polished written one. But because the talks were largely delivered extemporaneously, then captured by audio transcription, that revision seemed inauthentic. Likewise, I fear many of the illustrations from current events may now be lost on the reader. As much as anything this last worries me. It's hard to recreate the feelings and moods of the first decade of this millennium unless one was there. And it's hard to share the emotional tone of a student body moving through those events, or the more local events of our close community, unless one was there. And of course, to the extent many of these events and illustrations are autobiographical, it was difficult enough to share them with my students then, much less with the distant reader now. Finally, because our community at Greenville was explicitly and unapologetically Christian, the value framework and even exhortations for response are unapologetically Christian. Some readers may find them indelicate or even repugnant. For all these limitations, I apologize. The talks were hardly brilliant then, perhaps even less so now. But I lay them out, twenty years later, as the musings of an old man who cared about students the best he could.

My thanks go to all the students and faculty who walked the walk and talked the talk with me during those ten years. They endured my leadership, and even my lectures in our senior Capstone course. They shared my joy in times of campus success and shared my pain in times of community hard times as well as my own deep personal loss.

Thank you!

Jim Mannoia
December 2020

INTRODUCTION

PARADOX AND VIRTUE

*"Most really important things in life are paradoxical.
This is the human condition.
Learning to embrace them is a rare virtue."*

The problem with physics...

It had been a long long night when I finally got up from my desk in my "coffin single" room in Senior House just a few yards from the bank of the Charles River across from Boston. I took the small step to my single bed, knelt down and put my head between my hands and squeezed. It was an effort to stay awake, and somehow it seemed it might help to squeeze my brain in order to pull together the complicated ideas I had been wrestling with for hours. It was for a sixty-page paper in one of only two courses in philosophy I took as an undergraduate. But it was my best, albeit naïve attempt to capture the conundrum I was seeing in my study of physics.

From the time of René Descartes (seventeenth century) and Isaac Newton (eighteenth century) light was taken to be a collection of "corpuscles" or particles. But by the nineteenth century, a famous experiment by Thomas Young shining light through first a single and then a double slit, showed that it behaved more like a wave, creating interference patterns impossible if it were a stream of particles. But then by the twentieth century, the photoelectric effect showed that when dimmed down enough, light does indeed come in discrete packages which would be impossible if it were a wave. The quandary baffled the best of minds from Albert Einstein to Richard Feynman who delighted in the impossibility of it all. Today quantum theory embraces both the particle *and* wave theories of light to account for such observations.

But such apparent contradiction was not limited to the wave particle nature of light. Similar dilemmas faced physicists attempting to pin down the location and velocity of particles in their high energy experiments. As it turns out, even contemporary physics in the twenty-first century recognizes that some "properties" are "incompatible;" they cannot both be known at the same time with equal precision. "Their operators do not commute."

The only conclusion that could be drawn was that apparently, some of our theories, like the "wave theory" and the "particle theory," while useful, do not give us a complete picture of reality. And in fact, the competing pictures they give may actually be contradictory. But surely "reality" is not confused or self-contradictory! Reality is what it is and apparently only our understanding is temporarily or even perhaps ultimately inadequate. What we have come to realize from this, is that our theories are merely limited frameworks for grappling with what is apparently a more complex reality than our theories can capture.

The familiar analogy sometimes used to illustrate this point reminds me of my days walking in Mana Pools, an amazing "Eden like" park on the shores of the Zambezi River in northern Zimbabwe. To a blind man, encountering an elephant for the first time, and grasping its tail, an elephant is "rope like" and the man might be tempted to apply his experience with ropes such as "having two ends" to the elephant. But another blind woman grasping the ears might be tempted to apply her knowledge of large plant leaves, or another blind person grasping the legs might imagine the properties of trees would apply broadly. And so it goes on with any limited experience of the elephant's trunk or tusk, or tongue, or bellowing. Some of these theories might even seem to contradict one another in an impossible way. But of course, the elephant is not impossible. Instead, it is the limitations of the restrictive theories we bring to our understanding that make it seem that way.

To pick on a different animal, it is said that the eyesight of a bee, created by a compound image from 7,000 to 9,000 separate facets, and receptors that detect ultraviolet colors but not red, "paints" quite a different "picture" of the world than our human vision. Which is right, ours or theirs? Of course, the answer is neither. We are each "asking different questions," and compiling the results of those "questions" into a different "answer" that is itself shaped by our interests. The urge to decide which is more true is beside the point.

So, it became clear to me as a student of physics that *perhaps* it's not so much that we don't yet have the answer to whether light is a particle or a wave, but rather that we are asking the wrong questions. Nature is not obliged to answer our specific questions; i.e., to fit Herself into our limited categories. She is not obliged to *have* a specific nature (particle or wave) or a specific location or velocity. Rather, it is our obligation to continue to ask different questions, create different categories, and hopefully create more complete, more comprehensive accounts for what Nature has been all along. And this may go on forever!

As a senior student of physics, I concluded that there may well always be an "essential tension" in our understanding of the world. And if this were true of the physical world, that principle may well extend to all human understanding. This idea, arising that night squeezing my head and reading an old medieval view called "Molinistic Partitionism," has come to echo throughout and even to permeate my thinking about most important truths.

Things are complicated...

In one sense this "tension" might be just an obvious principle that we all readily accept. "Things are complicated" and most of the theories/ constructions/frameworks/explanations we use in everyday "accounting for things" can only go so far. Beyond that, the accounts are just too simple. But this leaves open the possibility that a better/more complete account will one day capture *all* those anomalies. This is optimistic/progressive. Or it may also just be another way of restating the aphorism that we should take "everything in moderation," including our explanations. Virtuous explanation is just a mean between vicious ones as Aristotle might say. But there may also be a deeper reason why this tension exists in so many accounts of the world. It may be that the highest/most complete way of knowing does not *allow* resolution of the dissonance but always and forever requires an embrace of multiple alternative and sometimes conflicting accounts to be held simultaneously. It may be about holding multiple points of view at once without resolving them into a single focus.

Francis Bacon (*Novum Organon*) says the human intellectual enterprise is always to resolve the cognitive dissonance (lack of fit) between our observations and our theories. These theories, Idols of the Tribe, the Den, the Market, or the Theater, provide the questions we ask. But should we encounter in the world, elements that do not fit these theories, we will be stymied. And the effort to *resolve* this dissonance may keep us from embracing a reality that *does not* fit or *does not yet* fit or *will not ever* fit any framework we may devise. This is not to say that those who embrace the highly successful empirical method should refrain from expanding their questions, their theories, their categories to capture a wider set of observations. The empirical method embodied in science has been highly successful and is probably our current most highly regarded form of knowledge. But there may be elements of reality that will never fit a single coherent set of categories. It may be that we must learn to embrace the contradictions in our own theories and benefit from what each side teaches us.

Consider this conclusion from another angle. For centuries in Western philosophy, the dominant paradigm for "knowing something" was "discovery." That is, learners were explorers looking to discover the true form of the world. Whether in science or geography or history, it was all about finding what was really there. But as the sequence from Descartes to Locke to Berkeley and Hume showed, we cannot escape our subjective contribution to knowing; our own point of view makes a difference. Just as modern physicists learned that the very act of observing a particle to find its location would alter its velocity (momentum), so modern epistemology came to understand that the true reality "out there" to be discovered, could never be reconciled, or connected in reliable correspondence to any theory. The result was skepticism. But Kant embraced this situation and made it explicit. Just as many say that the history of philosophy is a series of footnotes to Plato, postmodern philosophy is a series of variations on Kant. From radical atheistic existentialism to higher biblical criticism, we are unavoidably limited by our subjectivist point of view. Notwithstanding divine Revelation to the contrary, even Christians confess that for now, "we see through a glass darkly." For now, this is simply the human condition.

How we sort things out...

We all hold a collection of observations, personal experiences, and beliefs close to our heart. Thoughtful people spend their lives searching either to find or construct a metanarrative (worldview) that makes sense of the largest number of the most important elements of this collection. Our efforts are not so different from those of scientists who, as T. Kuhn, I. Lakatos, and others suggest, are sometimes forced to throw out some of what does not "fit." Less thoughtful people simply live with open contradictions they do not see or about which they care very little. More thoughtful people struggle their entire lives in a kind of internal intellectual battle that exhausts them as they leap in perpetual agnosticism from alternative to variation in search of a framework to reconcile it all. Some of these lose their minds. More radical people embrace the contradictions and explicitly reject rationality, putting choice ahead of truth, existence ahead of essence. Wittgenstein said of that whereof we cannot speak (rationality) we must remain silent. Still others, and this is the view I take, hold very lightly to their theories, recognizing them for what they are: merely human lenses catching what light is available to understand and live "reasonably" (sic!). Yet this humble epistemological stance does not make them less passionate. Such a person is both epistemologically humble *and* committed (even passionate) because they understand the human condition yet embrace a framework of the world that affirms it has meaning beyond that condition.

There is a tempting mistake in most of these responses. It is tempting to suppose that because we cannot discover or construct the complete theory, the complete framework, the complete metanarrative or world view, that there either *is* no reality outside our constructions, or that if there is, it has no structure/meaning. If we cannot be absolutely sure of Truth, but only construct our little truths, then there simply *is* no Truth. But why should that be? Why take such a plunge, a little like Berkeley? He said since we cannot *know* the primary or secondary qualities of things outside our minds; since we cannot know what that external reality is like, that there can *be* no grounds for saying there *is* a Reality, a Truth, outside ourselves. Why not instead, just say that while we cannot know that Reality, that Truth, in a way that forces It to submit to our theories, our formulations, our heuristics, we can *still* believe (and perhaps with rational warrant) that there is a Reality, a Truth with which we can live because we hold it is only "knowable" through embracing a paradoxical tension.

So, apologetics (for any theory, be it scientific, religious, or political) should come down to no more and no less than asking whether the conceptual framework we use to make sense of our own collection of experiences and beliefs is *adequate* for our collection, *reasonable* (free of logical contradiction), and *coherent* so far as we can tell. When anomalies arise, thoughtful people simply make adjustments and move on, maximizing gain and minimizing loss of meaning or purpose.

Consequently, some of the elements of our conceptual framework will be fundamental and others merely auxiliary hypotheses (Lakatos). If necessary, we will tinker with these latter first before questioning the former. Conversion (even religious conversion) becomes a matter of shifting our framework, our paradigm, in substantial ways.

In short, we are all "game players." We "play" the serious lifelong game of seeking and constructing frameworks to make the most sense of our collections about the world. Now it is tempting to suppose this makes the game frivolous, unimportant, a waste of time. I have heard this objection from many thoughtful friends, especially about philosophy. Nothing could be further from what I am claiming. This is a noble game, among the highest in which humans can engage. It is what we do! And for those of us who believe there is Beauty and Truth, even if it is always just beyond our ability to fully grasp it, this "game" is our worship, our homage, our actualization. We need not suppose a fine carpenter is producing the perfect table to believe she is exercising noble skills. And it is not even necessary to say the effort must make progress, though it is tempting to suppose in some cases it does. Perhaps, and even probably, science today offers improved frameworks for understanding, coping with, and even manipulating the physical world. If there are "laws of nature," or "patterns of regular divine activity" in the world, science may today understand those patterns better than ever. Science may "make better sense" of the largely shared "collection of experiences and beliefs about the physical world." But progress is an elusive mistress as experiences and beliefs that must be adequately accommodated may change from age to age. Natural physical phenomena and even our personal spiritual, moral, and intellectual environment may change so that the frames we need to make sense of them may have to change or be adjusted too.

So, it should not be surprising that human efforts/theories/frameworks to understand the world, whether physical or nonphysical are fraught with apparent contradictory perspectives, seemingly opposing points of view, that nevertheless add to our understanding and particularly our ability to cope with life. This is what I mean by paradox. It is a rare virtue to embrace it; and virtues themselves usually embody it.

Paradox...

If we were to look for definitions of "paradox" we would find many. At a very simple level, some might say that calling something paradoxical just means we haven't figured it out yet

Another conversational view is that "paradox" refers to statements that are ironic or unexpected, such as "the paradox that standing is more tiring than walking." That is, it seems it can be either: Appears right but can't be, or appears wrong but is true.

Another example ties us to the starting point of this chapter. Paradox is "a potentially serious conflict between quantum mechanics and the general theory of relativity known as the information paradox."

A more developed view is that "A paradox is a statement that apparently contradicts itself and yet at the same time might still be true (or false). For many decades teaching logic, I always insisted that if an argument led to a contradiction (*reduction ad absurdum*) that proved the premises were not all true. But this rule only applies to logics which are bivalent; i.e., allow only two values, True and False. However, life is not that simple.

A weaker variation, amenable to doxastic logics, is that a paradox is a statement or proposition that, despite sound (or apparently sound) reasoning from acceptable premises, leads to a conclusion that *seems* senseless, logically unacceptable, or self-contradictory. This makes no simple claim to the truth or falsity of the conclusion, nor by extension to the premises, but only that we are baffled about what to believe and with how much certainty.

So what?...

So, in one sense the thesis of this book, that most really important things in life are paradoxical, is obvious, and to some uninteresting. It sounds a bit like "we can't be absolutely sure about anything (other than definitions)." So, let's all just "take a little of this and a little of that," or walk the moderate line, pursuing the Aristotelian mean. Maybe this is all there is to it and my effort here is kicking a dead horse or preaching to the choir. Maybe pervasive paradox is just "obvious?!" Some may say "Of course!" If so, I apologize, maybe it's just taken me seventy years to see this clearly.

But to my mind, it is our failure to understand this, to fall instead into either/or, win/lose dualisms with dogmatic even fanatic zeal, that artificially creates division, pits us against one another, forces us to take sides, distracts us from focusing on where we agree, destroys civility, polarizes opinion, and prevents the honest dialogue that can truly improve our understanding of and ability to cope with the world around us.

Now of course the radical subjectivists among us will not object. They will smile and say "Welcome to reality…(sic!)" They may even opine that my claim that there *are* any "most important things in life" is presumptuous! I can't and won't argue. But for them I only wish a world in which either everyone agrees with them or one in which their opinion is also held by those in power.

But for those who object that there is Truth, that the fundamental tenets of their world view, even their faith, require them to insist that there is Truth, and that at least to some degree we can know it, I must say more. The view I hold does not deny that there is Truth beyond our constructions. It does not even deny that there may be supernatural aspects of our knowing process. There may be divine revelation, both natural and special. In fact, I believe in both. That is part of my framework for understanding the world as an orthodox follower of Jesus Christ. But the fact that I believe there is Truth, and even in a special way of accessing this Truth, does not mean I can avoid the inevitable problem of the human condition. I *cannot* do more than see through a glass darkly. I *cannot* avoid the interpretive moment in receiving and understanding that Truth even through Revelation. In particular, despite belief, and divinely inspired faith in the uniqueness of biblical revelation, I believe it must still be interpreted using the best exegetical and hermeneutical frameworks we can discover/construct with God's help. Facts and propositions do not speak for themselves. What is more, acknowledging a theological insight of neoorthodoxy, even if propositions *did* speak for themselves, the Truth is not a particular proposition so much as a Person.

So, what follows are talks to young students attempting to help them understand that the moral life is not simple. In each talk I have tried to describe a virtue, to illustrate it from then current events around the world in our own community and my own life, and when possible, to point out that virtue is often paradoxical. Virtues demand that we embrace apparent contradictions, that simple formulas are rarely enough, that living the moral life will require a crucial balancing act, an essential tension, an embracing of paradox. And in particular, I sought to illustrate that the moral life of following Jesus Christ will require a paradoxical balance of passionate commitment *and* epistemological humility available only with intentional self-conscious effort and discipline to meet and trust the Person who is Himself Truth. Hence the title of this short book, *Paradox and Virtue*.

ONE

A LIBERATING PARADOX

SEPTEMBER 9, 1999

It's good to see all of you here this morning. September is always an exciting time as the campus fills up again for a new academic year. You bring an energy to campus when all of you come back. But I think this past weekend was perhaps full of adrenaline, and maybe today that rush is wearing off a little. You are beginning to think about classes and remembering, or for freshmen, beginning to realize, that work is involved here.

Last spring, I had the privilege of speaking to you on three separate occasions. And each time I talked to you I said that I had intended to talk to you about my philosophy of education. Yet each time I diverted from that and didn't really do it. Nevertheless, at the end of each of those talks I pointed out that a theme of "paradox" had emerged, and because of that, in a way, I *had* been talking about my philosophy of education. Well, today I would like to try actually to say a few things about what I think this whole college learning process is about. So, I don't have an inspirational talk for you today, I don't have a sermon for you today, I don't have a devotional for you today. Instead, I'd like to ask you to think hard with me and use this as an occasion to reflect on the process we are beginning here together. I want to talk about why I think a *liberal arts education* is so distinctive.

You have heard that phrase many times before and some of you may realize you are paying "bigger bucks" to get a liberal arts education instead of that often quite different one from a state university somewhere. As a result, it seems to me it is important for you to understand what is really different about it. Now what I am going to say in the next couple of minutes is probably the key. So, if you want to go to sleep, do it after this.

The liberal arts are important and distinctive for at least two reasons. First, often we ask the question, "What does this education that I'm getting do for me?" And that's a very important one to ask! What does the education do for you? It prepares you for life in practical ways. At Greenville we call that "service." In other words, this education has what I elsewhere call an *instrumental* value (*Christian Liberal Arts: An Education that Goes Beyond*). This is a value that helps you to go out and do something else better. That's the side of education that most of us think about and most of our parents think about because they don't want you living at home at the age of thirty-five taking the trash out for an allowance. And neither do you. But second, we shouldn't just be asking, "What is the practical, the instrumental value of a liberal arts education?" We should also be asking, "What is its intrinsic value?" Another way of putting this is, you shouldn't just ask what this education is going to do for me. You should also ask what this education going to do to me. "What will it do to me inside?" At Greenville we sometimes say this is an education for service, yes, but also an education for character.

Now if you don't remember anything else this morning, remember that. As you freshmen begin or you upper classmen continue this educational process, what I'm going to call an educational exodus, try to ask yourself this year, next year, every semester, "What is this education doing for me," but equally, "What is it doing to me?" What value does it have by itself, regardless of how practical or impractical it might be? That distinction is what makes the education here at Greenville different.

Now I want to say a few things first, about the practical side, the service side. Because in fact that side is also different at Greenville from what you would get from other places. We want you to leave with more than just basic cultural knowledge, or even basic disciplinary skills from whatever major you choose to pursue. We want you also to leave with transferable skills like reading, writing, thinking, researching, and collaborating. These are very important because they will help you not just with your first job, but through the six careers you are likely to undertake in a lifetime. And finally, we want you to be able to approach real world problems in an integrative way. That's different from the kind of narrow specialization you might get in other colleges and universities. So even this practical side, the "What's it doing for me?" side is different here. And I plan to talk to you more about that later in the semester.

But today I want to talk especially about what we hope this education is doing to you. I want to focus on this in part because it is a lot less common and in part because it is a lot more important in our society today. It is character formation. You don't have to watch the news very much to realize that our society needs people who are more than just practically trained.

We need people who have character. What then does character formation look like? How *does* this education *do* something to me? In a way the answer is a story about a journey.

Yesterday Dr. [Randall] Balmer talked about "Journeying Mercies." And today, in a way I want to talk about a journey too. Except I want to use the story of the Exodus, the story of the Exodus of the people of God. Because you see all of us are involved in a character forming process that is like an exodus. All of us are on this journey. Some of you are just beginning, some of you are seniors, and some of you are adults who have followed this journey for many, many years. But we are all on this road. And it is a process that goes through stages. Faculty can give you much more detail than I about developmental psychology and point you to the works of Kohlberg, Piaget, Gilligan, Fowler, and others like them, who describe the ways in which we develop and grow.

But in a nutshell, I'd like to suggest that all of us go through a journey of intellectual, moral, and spiritual development. Roughly speaking I'd like to describe it in three stages. First is a stage where everything seems quite clear, even black and white. That's what a high school mindset is often like. And there is nothing wrong with that. Don't misunderstand. We all have to start the journey. Everything is black and white. Typically, a person who is in this stage of development is very passionate, very sure, and very committed to things. He or she believes everything one-hundred percent; but sometimes to the point of dogmatism. It is however a natural stage of intellectual, moral, and spiritual development.

Often in college years—and these are critical years in this journey—you move to a stage that is no longer black and white. You begin to realize things are "gray." You learn to appreciate shades of meaning and even truth. That stage is characterized no longer by a kind of passionate one-hundred percent commitment that becomes dogmatic, but instead, to put it positively, by a kind of open-mindedness. Often however, it becomes a kind of skepticism or even cynicism. You know what I am talking about, right? In fact, the word *sophomore* sometimes defines this stage. "Well," they say, "you do your thing and I'll do mine. Everybody's opinion is as good as anybody else's." It sounds like stereotypes of California. As in the book of Judges, "Everyone did what was right in their own eyes" (Judges 21:25 NASB). That is a second stage.

But I think there is a third stage, and I like to call it "critical commitment." It is a stage where people are committed like the first stage *and* open-minded like the second stage, but unlike either stage they are neither dogmatic nor skeptical. This stage, this place in your journey, is what I would yearn for all of you. And I hope you will begin to see and understand this journey that you undertake and begin even now, even today.

Now, really, I could stop there. But I want to illustrate this largely theoretical account from the historical Exodus. You all know the story. The people of God living in Palestine faced a famine. Joseph was sold into slavery, winds up in Egypt and becomes a powerful leader. His father sends his brothers down there to find some food. You know what happened. The people of God wind up living in Egypt for a long, long time. However, eventually God calls them out, and at first, they are afraid, looking into the wilderness between them and their destination. They are worried, even scared. Eventually, like you, they begin their journey, and it is really tough. They wander for forty years and a lot of them are lost and die in the wilderness. But they persist and do arrive in the Promised Land. It's a familiar story.

In many ways, the educational "exodus" that you are undertaking today is like that Exodus. There are some powerful analogies that I'd like you to consider and remember as we go forward. First of all is Goshen. They started in Goshen, the Nile-Delta, the northern part of Egypt. It was "OK" for the people of God to be there. It is "OK" for a high school graduate to be a black and white thinker who is committed and passionate, maybe even a little dogmatic, seeing everything as right or wrong. It's like my student in philosophy class who after I have argued two sides of an issue raises their hand and asks, "Would you just tell me what the right answer is?" That is black and white thinking, "us and them" thinking. There is nothing wrong with that. But it is just where we start. So, the people of God started in the land of Goshen. They were supposed to be there. That had been God's plan earlier to save the people.

But sometimes God calls you to move out, and apparently, he has called you to move out or you wouldn't be in college. At such a time, like God's people in Egypt, you first have a responsibility to step out, to leave. And for those who are called out, to leave is liberation.

Second, when you move out, you leave your comfort zone. Think about the people of God. Did they really want to leave? They moaned and groaned and complained. Yes, they were slaves; oppressed. But when Moses said, "Let's get out of here!", they said, "Well to where!?" And he said, "Out there!" And where did he point? He pointed out into the desert. Now to them, that didn't look particularly comfortable. It didn't look like a lot of fun. Likewise, if we are called to go out, we are called to leave our comfort zone.

How many of you have ever served on an athletic team? I see a lot of raised hands. In sports, athletes, coaches and even parents understand a pretty important principle. And it is a simple principle. "No pain no gain!" If you have worked hard at athletics, then you know that you only grow when you stretch just a little bit beyond where you were the last time. Right? If you aren't stretching, then you aren't growing. "No pain no gain!" And every good coach knows that he or she has got to stretch the athlete, push them just a little bit farther.

Now if that principle works for physical development, why should it be any different for intellectual development, moral development, even spiritual development? No pain no gain! If you are going to undertake this journey, this educational "exodus," then leaving the land of Goshen to be liberated, means leaving your comfort zone. So, you have to deliberately, willfully, and continuously seek out occasions where you are going to be stretched. Right? Doesn't that make sense?! Isn't that what you are here for?!

Third, the people of God didn't just walk into the desert pain by themselves. They followed a leader. They followed Moses. At first, they were not sure about him. But in the end, I think they figured it made sense to have a leader. Still, sometimes they trusted him and sometimes they didn't. Right?

But who was this guy? First of all, he was a guy that was educated and grew up in Pharaoh's family. That helped. Second, he was experienced. He was experienced in the wilderness. Moses had had his own time of wandering in the wilderness doubting. But God had brought him out of it. So, he was educated and he was experienced. Yet, he was also humble. Scripture tells us that Moses was the meekest man on earth. Now *meek* sounds like he was a wimp! Who wants to follow a meek leader? But *meek* doesn't mean weak. *Meek* means someone who is powerful, but who has channeled it; in this case in the way God wanted it to be channeled. It is like a powerful river that would be wild but instead it is dammed up and now serves a useful purpose. So, the people of God followed Moses. He was educated, experienced, and humble. You are undertaking an educational "exodus" here at Greenville. I hope and pray the faculty at Greenville College are likewise educated, experienced, and humble. Leave the land of Goshen, get out of your comfort zone, follow the leaders.

What happened to the people of God? They took a risk. They wandered and it wasn't easy. I'd like to put a sign outside on the street in front of the college. A sign below the one that reads "Greenville College." This sign would add two lines, "Enter at Your Own Risk," "There is education going on here!" Not training, but education; liberating education. Greenville College is not an entirely safe place. The wilderness was not an entirely safe place. People got lost out there. This means if you came here because you wanted to be safe, then beware, because it is not entirely so. If an educational exodus involves spiritual, moral, and intellectual pilgrimage you can get lost. Now we pray to God that you won't. But Greenville College is not an entirely safe place. You have to understand that there are risks involved because it's education that is going on. If you are moving from the land of Goshen, if you are to be liberated and headed to the "Promised Land," you have to take some risks. The people of God understood that. You should understand that. Leave Goshen, leave your comfort zone, follow your leaders, and take some risks.

Thank God that it is not just Moses leading or even just the faculty at Greenville College. Ultimately, God is leading, and God is involved. Think about His people back then. How were they led? God supplied their food; the manna and meat. He supplied their water. Moses hit rocks and it gushed out. God supplied it. And perhaps most importantly, He supplied direction; the pillar of fire by night and the cloud by day. Isn't that right? It wasn't just Moses, it was divine leadership!

Now keep in mind that God's leadership in your life is not something that you will necessarily see next week. He didn't tell the people of God where he wanted them to go the next week and give them a map. He just put the fire pillar and the column of clouds there, and they followed it day by day. Sometimes it moved, sometimes it didn't. They didn't have it all mapped out in advance. God's guidance doesn't work that way. So, if you wonder what your major is going to be or where this doubt will lead you that is creeping into your journey, this question, this risk, this tough time, remember, the people of God didn't know from week to week. They only knew one day at a time. And he provided one day at a time for them.

Leave Goshen, get out of your comfort zone, follow the leader, take a risk, rest on God's guidance, and finally, live in community. The people of God didn't make this journey all by themselves, individually, one after the other. Did they? They did it together and it was a big crowd. This college too is a community of scholarship, a place where we care about intellectual, spiritual, moral, and social development. We do it together. Think about the people of God and the Exodus. It wasn't Moses alone especially in the battles. Remember when they were going to battle against the Ammonites. Did Moses go down and wield the sword? No, he didn't. He was an old man. He sent Joshua. Now Joshua was one ripped guy. But Joshua couldn't do it by himself either. He couldn't even do it with all of the soldiers he had. God had to help. Remember, God told Moses to raise up his hands. He raised up his hands; but not for very long. He grew weak and tired. So, who did he get to help him? Two younger guys, Aaron and Hur. They held up his old arms. Moses couldn't even talk very well. So, Aaron did a lot of talking for him. And Moses couldn't do all the judging either! His father-in-law Jethro said, "Get some guys to help you." This was a community project. They needed each other. You need each other. In your educational exodus you need the people sitting next to you. In particular, you need people who think differently from yourself. In other words, find the people who don't think the way you think. Talk to them and listen to them and they will stretch you and help you to grow. Living in community means living with diversity, and that is good and helps you make the trip.

Leave Goshen, get out of your comfort zone, follow the leader, take a risk, let God lead, live in community, and finally, you will enjoy the fruit and will enter the "land" God has promised for you. Some of you will take four years, some five, I hope none of you will take forty years. But you will enter the land promised. What will it be like? What was the Promised Land like? It was great. A land filled with milk and honey. It was wonderful. It was freedom. Liberation leads to freedom. But freedom involves responsibilities. The people of God did not have an altogether easy time, even in the Promised Land. Don't assume that your problems will be over when you get a college degree. But they will be different problems because critical commitment, as I have described it, requires attention. And it is not easy. There will be temptations and difficulties. To be a liberally educated person, to be liberated and to live in your "promised land" is not easy because it involves embracing paradox. You have heard me talk about this before. It means believing, but not being sure. It means being passionate, but open-minded. It means taking a position, but listening to other people with an attitude of humility that characterizes critical commitment. Those are what we learn from the Exodus.

In summary, what does it require of you? It requires of you to risk and to trust. To risk leaving where you have been in a high school way of thinking that was altogether appropriate. To risk leaving your comfort zone by trusting the leadership, trusting the faculty, and above all by trusting God. What does it require for you faculty? It requires that you be willing to provoke, push, prod, and to stretch deliberately to make your students' lives a little uncomfortable. You are the coaches! If you are not stretching them, then no one will. But it also means for you to embrace them and nurture them in community. This means while students have to embrace the paradox of risk and trust, faculty have to embrace the paradox of provoking and nurturing. If we embrace and understand our task, we will move forward, and will undertake together to complete this grand educational "exodus."

TWO

VISION: TO SEE BUT NOT TO SEE

FEBRUARY 9, 1999

Not Seeing...

Over the past several weeks, I have spent a lot of time driving in blizzards, night and day, on ice and snow, headed east and headed west. The most recent stretch of course was the long pull from New York to Greenville in a two-car caravan lugging those parts of the family that would not have found the inside of the moving van hospitable to living creatures: people, plants, and even our black lab Fiel. And of course it happened smack in the middle of the snow storm of the decade! But there had been an earlier trip too. Our family gathered for the holidays at my son's bachelor condominium in downtown Minneapolis. New York to Minneapolis in the winter is a *long* seventeen hours! How many healthy rice cakes can you eat before the craving for real junk food wins out?! The trip back home to New York was even longer. Naturally, the after Christmas catch-up meant truck traffic was timed to match our travel. Every tractor trailer in America was on I-90 headed east that dark snowy night. It seemed my wipers had been shipped from England on the Mayflower, and when I replaced them, the new ones immediately froze up. What's more, the heavy wind caught them enough on every sweep to lift them off the window leaving an opaque band of dried salt precisely at eye level. To make matters worse, it seemed that every time I pulled alongside the biggest tractor trailers and reached that critical moment of blindness puncturing the truck's bow wave of muddy spray, the left lane would get icy and the washer fluid reservoir would dribble and plug up!

To put this all another way, over the past several weeks changing homes and changing jobs has forced me to spend a lot of time thinking about vision—wishing I could *see* more clearly. Maybe you have felt the same way these days. Whether you have braved the wintry interstates or debated what major you would like to choose, or even just worried what you will do when you graduate in May, you may also have been thinking about vision.

My training is in physics and in philosophy. In physics I specialized in optics, which means I spent a lot of time huddled in a very dark lab thinking a lot about light. As a philosopher, I specialized in metaphysics, which means I spent a lot of time wrestling in the dark with a lot of definitions, wishing I had some light! Naturally, both these experiences affect my thinking and what I would like to say about vision. And one inclines me to the practical, the other to the theoretical!

That word *vision* reveals an interesting ambiguity. Often it refers to the *result* of seeing. It is a kind of mental picture; as in "I saw a vision," or "Heather is a vision." At other times it refers to the *capacity* to see, as in "I had the optometrist check my vision," or "Owls have amazing night vision." And sometimes this ambiguity can get confusing. On the highway that night a few weeks ago I had my vision but sure wished I had a vision. I could see but sure wished I could see. I think you get the picture here, right?

So maybe, like me, you sometimes get confused and wonder if you have vision at all. You believe you can see but you can't really see. It may be that you do have the capacity to see, but you just can't see the picture. I would like to suggest two reasons why this sometimes happens, why it is okay, and what we can do about it.

It's too DARK...

Sometimes, those with good vision cannot see because it is too dark.

That night returning from Minneapolis to New York, we had been driving thirteen hours already. Chicago was history and Cleveland was ahead. Moisture laden air over warm Lake Erie was driving prevailing northwesterly winds back over cold northern Ohio. The temperature dropped through the dewpoint like an express elevator and with it dropped tons of lake effect snow. It was very dark. At first, we moved ahead; not at all sure where we were going. I used all the tricks. Living in western New York—"lake effect heaven"—you learn them well. They are survival skills! And they are all good advice for people with vision who cannot see. First, you don't change directions too quickly. Second, you slow down. Third, you look out the windows to the sides to gauge the road. And fourth, at least if you're a former physicist, you may even try to imagine how the tires are "feeling."

But above all, fifth, you keep moving. Sometimes it takes great courage to keep moving. Whether it is passing a tractor trailer in a blizzard at night or just getting up on those dark mornings when your vision is faded, it takes courage to keep moving because you wonder if you really can still see.

By about 9 p.m., we realized we were alone on the road. At the next rest area, we pulled in and discovered where everyone had gone. The whole of I-90 was already there! We talked to others, we listened, and we weighed our options. Again, each of these is good advice for people with vision who cannot see. But in the end, we did *not* move ahead; we waited. We stayed a while at the rest stop, then crawled ahead slowly a mile or two to an exit without knowing for sure where we were going. We found a motel and waited again—this time, reluctantly, overnight. We still had a clear vision of our home in Houghton 250 miles ahead. But for the time being, because we could not see, we needed to wait. As we waited, we hoped we would see more clearly tomorrow. And we did. The day was clear, and we moved forward again, all the way home. So sometimes, when we have vision but cannot see, it takes courage to move ahead. But sometimes, it takes a different kind of courage to wait; not sure of where we are going.

Abraham understood this lesson of moving and waiting in the dark. When God called him out of the land of his ancestors, he moved ahead obediently even when he couldn't see where he was going. In the selection from Hebrews (11:8 RSV) we just read, we are told, "By faith Abraham obeyed when called to go out to a place which he was to receive as an inheritance; and he went out not knowing where he was to go." Because he had vision, Abraham courageously moved ahead even when he could not see.

But that is not the end of the story, or of Abraham's courage for that matter. The account in Genesis (15:12) makes it clear that moving ahead even for Abraham was not an easy matter. We all recall the famous passage recounting his faithful obedience; "He believed the Lord and it was reckoned to him as righteousness" (Romans 4:3 RSV). Yet within only a few verses, we are told that a dread and great darkness fell upon him. Even with fresh vision, like Abraham, we can grow discouraged and depressed. Perhaps you have known that feeling and the fear that you have lost your vision in the dark.

In this case Abraham was also expected to show the courage to wait. God had given him the capacity to see, but only to see a very few details. It was vision for a Promised Land and Abraham had moved ahead without knowing where he was going. But God had also given a vision for his offspring, an entire nation, who would number with the stars of heaven; and Abraham was already seventy-five years old! Twenty-four years later, Abraham still had his vision, but God had not given him the picture. For twenty-four years in the dark, he had waited. It is tough to wait that long and pretty easy to try to do things your own way (think of Hagar), or to grow cynical—even if you are Abraham. In fact, after all those years, when God reminded him of the promise (Genesis 17:1–8), we are told "Abraham fell on his face and laughed" (v. 7, RSV).

Now I think this is great! There are not that many places in the Bible where we read about laughter. Can you see the picture here? He has been promised a huge family. But he has been waiting longer than most of you have been alive! And now Abe is ninety-nine years old! Keep in mind this is before the days of Viagra. He is not just amused, but I get the impression from the account that he thinks God's reminder is hysterical. He falls on his face laughing. When you are ninety-nine years old you do not fall on your face too frequently or too casually…you might not get back up. In fact, I imagine old Abe is actually on the ground rolling around laughing. "Riiiiight Lord! Give me a break! You have gotta be kidding!"

But the story gets better. Apparently, Abraham has not told his wife Sarah about this vision for a promised nation, or for that matter, about the reminder and the laughing episode twenty-four years later. I suppose you can understand why not. She's ninety years old herself. You might say Abraham has vision but again, he just can't see it happening, so there's no use stirring up trouble with someone [his wife!] who would obviously have to play a pretty big part in making it happen!

In any case, sometime later, the Lord returns, this time meeting Abraham under the oaks at Mamre, and reminds him again of the vision. This time Sarah is listening at the door. Now it's her turn to laugh. Scripture tells us she at least had the decency not to roll around on the ground doing it in God's very presence. It says she "laughed to herself" saying, "After

I have grown old, and my husband is old, shall I have pleasure" (Genesis 18:12 NRSV)? Unfortunately, discretion doesn't work when the jokester is omniscient! God responds, as if offended, asking Abraham why his wife laughed? God seemed to be asking, "Doesn't she think I can really do this?" Luckily for Abraham, Sarah jumps in. I mean, it's not my idea of fun to get into an argument with the Creator. As Jacob discovered, a body can get hurt! But unfortunately for Sarah, she was scared and that's exactly what she did. She said, "I didn't laugh!" and God replied, "Oh yes you did" (Genesis 18:15 NRSV)! Now there's no report on how long this "Yes you did!" "No, I didn't!" went on. Having raised two children of my own I can assure you it can go on a long time. But the fact is God had the final word. Within a year Isaac was born, and the rest is history—"heilsgeschicte"—"religious history" to be precise.

When neither of them could see, Abraham and Sarah had the vision and courage to wait. In the words of Oswald Chambers:

> When God gives a vision and darkness follows, wait…
> Never try and help God fulfil His word. Abraham waited
> through 24 years of silence, but in those years all self-
> sufficiency was destroyed; there was no possibility left
> of relying on common sense ways (*My Utmost*, 1/19).

I have one final thought about keeping our vision even when we cannot see in the dark. In 1969 I was an officer of the InterVarsity chapter at M.I.T. Following, perhaps, the example of the church at Antioch, the other officers felt led to appoint me as a missionary to begin an evangelistic Bible study in a dormitory where none of us lived and where we had no members. I posted some notices and soon was meeting in a basement lounge once a week with three or four students. The large lounge was empty and dark except for a recessed light that cast a narrow cone on our little group. Sometime later, for two or three weeks, a young man attended but despite our invitations to move in closer, sat just outside that cone of light. He was a self-confessed atheist and rarely said anything at all. He just listened. Now I wish I could tell you there is a happy ending to this story and the young man eventually joined us and came to know the Lord. The fact is that after one memorable night, I don't recall that he ever returned, and I never saw him again. That night the other students and I were having the perennial discussion, "How do you know God's will?" It was really just another variation on our focus today, on having vision even when you cannot see. We went through all the standard answers—pray, read scripture, ask advice from wise Christian friends, use your common sense. But those answers were not all that satisfying, and as our confidence ebbed away, that young atheist spoke out of the darkness, words I have never forgotten. They gave me reason for courage to move ahead and courage to wait, even when my vision does not let me see in the dark. He said, "You Christians sure are funny people. If God is really who you say he is, he is surely more than able to make His purposes plain. It seems to me you guys should just worry about making sure you can accept His will, whatever it turns out to be." Out of the mouths of donkeys, babes, and sometimes even atheists!

In the months of deliberation about coming to Greenville, I have sought to focus on submitting my will to His. And then, when it is dark and my vision does not let me see, I pray for courage to move ahead and courage to wait.

It's too LIGHT...

A few minutes ago, I promised to suggest two reasons why we sometimes get confused and wonder if we really do have vision; why we believe we can see but cannot now see. The first reason was that sometimes those with good vision cannot see because it is too dark. But at other times even with good vision, we cannot see because it is too light!

That night driving to Cleveland, I noticed ironically that occasionally I had to turn my headlights down. If you've ever driven in a blizzard you've probably noticed this yourself. The bright beams on heavy snow made it impossible to see. I confess that in New York I have sometimes driven with parking lights alone. My eyes were fine, but there was too much light.

Plato tells the story of a group of slaves born and raised in a dark cave. Chained so they cannot turn around, with their backs to the mouth of the cave, their only experience is with the gray two-dimensional shadows cast on a great inner wall by objects moving behind them which they cannot see. Because they know nothing more, they become "experts" at naming and even arguing with one another about the many shapes they see moving and changing across the great inner screen of their private world. When one day one of their company is liberated and emerges to face the full light of the sun, he is blinded and unable to see anything. He has vision but cannot see; in this case because it is too light. To those who live outside, he is a new fool unable to do even the simplest things in his new place. If he is patient and waits courageously, his eyes will adjust and the profound beauty of a three-dimensional world full of color will become plain to see. And of course, it is no use trying to return to his former friends still imprisoned in the cave. Were he to do so, his eyes, now accustomed to the bright light of the sun, would be useless in a dark cave and their complex questions about shadows would be impossible to answer. He would now appear as an old fool even in his old world.

Plato used his story to make a case for education. Seek the knowledge of the Good and you will escape the "blindness" of dark ignorance even if it means temporary blindness from the light of what you learn and the ridicule of others. But along with the early Christian interpreters of Plato, we can see how it is God, not just the Good we seek, even though we may for some time be blinded by His light. Again, in the words of Oswald Chambers, "As soon as God becomes real, other people become shadows...There is a darkness which comes from excess of light" (My Utmost, 1/19).

So today, we have vision. But though we have vision it may also be true we cannot see! His ways are not our ways (Isaiah 55:8). We see now only through a glass darkly (1 Corinthians 13:12). Whether blinded by darkness or blinded by light, the result is the same. The good news is we need not fear but take courage. With Abraham and Sarah, we need courage to move ahead and the courage to wait. One day, sooner or at least much later, we shall see.

For now, our task is to acknowledge our blindness. And that brings me to some closing thoughts. As you may have realized, all of this has been a form of personal confession; and maybe it is for you too. Coming to Greenville

College this month I have vision. My vision is for us to become a place where the life of the mind is pursued for the glory of God. Where faculty and students work together to become men and women of character and service. In character to become more than dogmatists and more than sceptics, but both passionate and self-critical in our commitment to Christ. In service, to be both equipped and motivated to address the real problems of our world with the spirit of a servant. This vision grips me at the heart of who I am and motivates me every day.

But though I have vision, it is also true that I have felt my blindness, felt my lack of courage, felt my brokenness and inadequacy. There are many challenges, some new and some longstanding. I suffer because I know that I will disappoint you, and dashed hopes are among life's greatest tragedies. Already I realize that in some cases I cannot see because it is too dark—I just don't have the information and perspective I need. But in other cases I can't see yet because it is too light—there are so many competing lights of opinion. Your brilliant welcome has been dazzling.

So, what am I to do? What are you to do? God gives us vision, but we can't yet see. "To see but not to see," that's the problem. In our blindness we must never underestimate Him who is our Vision. For over one hundred years Greenville College has been a place where people can confess their inadequacy and find courage from the Holy Spirit available through our community. Twenty-nine years ago, this week, revival swept our campus. The Holy Spirit met blindness and inadequacy with acceptance and openness.

At that time emeritus professor Jim Rheinhard wrote, "God made me very conscious of His acceptance of me, even while I am unacceptable, I accepted my acceptance." Professor Frank Thompson wrote:

> The Holy Spirit is working with unusual effect...[people] are being led to face their personal spiritual needs and to experience God's forgiveness and personal wholeness. Individuals have found a new ability to be honest with themselves and with God...In my life, the constant presence of the Holy Spirit as a person is bringing me new faith and strength and wonder and joy.

Rev. Herb Coates, then pastor in Vandalia, and sharing the platform with me today, said that week, twenty-nine years ago, "I sensed a deep peaceful contagious spirit of love...it was beautiful to see barriers of [all kinds] melt into insignificance." And a visiting professor from Brazil, a longtime personal friend of mine, Professor Yoshikazu Takyia, said a marvelous thing about Greenville College. He said, "It is *liberating* just coming here. [God's] forgiving grace, healing presence, *liberating* action are felt by just coming here."

That is the tradition of Greenville College. God's grace makes Greenville College a *liberating* place. And those same resources are available to me and to you today. The Holy Spirit is still alive and well among us. The Mid-Winter faculty staff retreat ended last week with a beautiful time of personal testimony and sharing. Some who have vision but cannot see, confessed. Others who have moved ahead or chosen to wait shared their insight, and everyone drew courage.

So today, as we begin a new semester, I ask you to pray. Pray for me, for yourself, and for Greenville College. Let us keep our eyes on Him and pray that His Holy Spirit will continue His historic endowment of vision even when we cannot see.

Let me close with the words of a Greenville student who sat where you are sitting only a few years ago:

> O gaze of love, so melt my pride, that I may in your house but kneel. And in my brokenness to cry spring worship unto thee, spring worship unto thee, spring worship unto thee"
> (Jars of Clay, "Hymn" from the album *Much Afraid* 1997).

THREE

GRACE: GOOD NEWS FOR LESLIE

MARCH 22, 1999

Introduction...

The last time I spoke to you, at the beginning of this semester, I talked to you about a kind of paradox, "To See But Not to See." I confess you will likely hear me say much about this theme over the months and years because I believe that learning to grapple with complexity, ambiguity, and apparent paradox is perhaps the single most essential element of a liberal arts education. So today I would like to talk about paradox again. This time it is about the absolutely mysterious, often scandalous, but wonderfully life-giving paradox of grace. I had originally intended to talk to you about my philosophy of education; to talk about the role of stretching ourselves intellectually, morally, and spiritually in order to grow. But then I met Leslie.

Leslie's Story...

It was a very long day for me last Friday. It started early, at 6:30 a.m. in the mountain valley of Kelowna, British Columbia. I ate breakfast with friends, behind broad picture windows looking out at what could have been a scene from a fantasy movie. The snowcapped Canadian Rockies plunged down to the mirror surface of Lake Okanaga. The sky was overcast, and lower clouds hung secretly in mountain passes, occasionally laying fingers on the lake. The geese drew V-shapes on the surface as they paddled silently within our view. But twelve hours later, the serenity and majesty had given way to exhaustion as I boarded the third flight of the day, this one from Detroit to St. Louis. I knew that even the hour-long flight would still leave me another hour's drive before I laid my head down in Joy House just a block from where I stand. When a fellow passenger noted that she was tired, having traveled already for twelve hours from Amsterdam, I marveled at just how far way British Columbia is from Greenville.

I first noticed Leslie as the flight attendants prepared to close the door and I heard a loud raspy female voice demanding that the pilot give us an update on the MSU/Oklahoma basketball score. She was a trim blond dressed in jeans and turtleneck, sporting a big green *SPARTAN* button. She was missing the game, and obviously not happy about it at all since apparently her sole purpose in making the trip was to cheer for her team. But it seemed that during her delay, she'd ended up in an airport bar with a wrestling team also coming to St. Louis. And it didn't take anyone on the plane long to figure out she was now very drunk and very loud. The flight attendant had threatened to throw her off the plane if she didn't behave. She had apparently agreed, but it obviously wasn't going to be easy.

As luck, or providence, would have it, she sat in the aisle seat across from my aisle seat, but just one row back. The wrestler behind me, and across from her, noted that once she settled into her seat, she immediately began to read a Bible. Almost inevitably, he inquired if she were religious. Wrong question! "No, I am not religious! No, I am not Christian! No, I am not Catholic, nor Protestant or anything else. I'm just a godly woman!" When Jason pressed her—you see we got to know one another quite well—alluding to her own drunken state and foul mouth, she made things much clearer, *and* much louder. "This Bible is the Word of God—Yes! the very Word of God! Yes, he wrote it! I believe this [slapping the Bible] only this and I base my life on it. Jesus died on the cross to save me from my sins and boy [she actually used significantly stronger language during the whole flight in fact] do I ever have a lot of them in my life. Religious people are always telling me I should get down on my knees and thank God for all the suffering in my life." Then using profanity, she concluded, "But my God isn't like that. He was sad about all my suffering."

For the next hour's flight, her story emerged, for everyone to hear whether they listened or not. Leslie was thirty-six years old, apparently a kindergarten teacher in a Michigan inner city school. The daughter of missionaries in the Far East, she is headed this coming Saturday to Russia to assist in translation for the pickup of adoptive children coming to families in the U.S. She knew suffering, she said, and in foul language made it clear to us all that she didn't think a lot of religious people did. Punctuating each question with vulgarity and profanity, she asked, "Have they ever been hit twice by drunk drivers and left likely never to walk again? Have they ever had a loaded gun stuck in their mouth? Have they ever been raped? Have they ever had their school kids pulled from closets where they'd been locked for days only to be hung to death by parents too high on cocaine to know the difference?" You get the picture! She was mad and had no time for religious people!

To these amazing stories, told I must say with the almost indubitable truth of the very drunk, she added two more. Cursing loudly, she asked, "Had those religious people ever known about these? Have they ever traded seats on a plane so a family could sit together in the row in front of her on a flight years back, then, when the plane crashed watched the family die before her eyes while she just walked out of the plane into an Iowa cornfield?"

But one last story obviously hurt the most. Thirteen years before, she and her college fiancé had been planning their December wedding. They had never argued before, but now were disagreeing about what flowers to use. He wanted roses, but she loved daisies. She insisted, "I've compromised enough, I want daisies." He left to drive around and cool off, saying he just might not come back. She said, "OK, so what do I care?" Three hours later, police informed her he had been found dying in an auto wreck, whispering her name and address. She announced to everyone on the plane that she has regretted those six words every day for the last thirteen years and she can never love that way again.

Leslie reported that her counselor—In her shoes who wouldn't have one?—told her she was bitter. She was also obviously angry, no doubt an outward defense against deep inner pain. But religious Christians told her suicide was a sin. Lacing her language with vulgarity, she told them she didn't believe that for one minute! Her God understood that, "You just wanted the hurt to stop." To be fair, Leslie admitted that perhaps the suffering of the other women in her Bible Study Fellowship might actually be more substantial than just the petty whining it appeared to be. But she just wished they wouldn't keep telling her to rejoice.

The conversation was not one sided. First, Leslie asked her seatmate. who turned out to be Katie, eagerly waiting to meet her boyfriend at the airport in St. Louis, what Katie thought about the Bible. Katie answered that it was God's Word, that she'd learned that in her Catholic confirmation classes.

But finally, when pressed, in a quiet voice, Katie shared that she trusted Christ as her savior. Intermixed with all her stories, and periodic whoops when the pilot reported the MSU score, Leslie interrogated the wrestler Jason behind me too. "What do you believe?" He said he was a Christian, to which she replied in a tone of voice with the controlled surgical precision of a theology professor or a very smart atheist, "And what does that mean!?" Big wrestler Jason replied, "Jesus is God and died for my sins." Leslie was impressed! And so was I!

Inevitably, Leslie noticed me. I had been writing thank you cards, listening over my shoulder. She commented on my handwriting; "You write beautifully. I've taught school for twelve years and there's no way I could ever write that beautifully. Would you write me a note?" I said I would, later. But she went on; "I noticed you were interested in our conversation back here. What do you believe?" Leslie is not only drunk; she is very smart and very perceptive. I told her that trusting and following Jesus was the most important thing in my life and that there is nothing we can do to deserve His love. Leslie agreed; "God accepts me where I am and takes me from there." "Christ died on the cross because people make mistakes. And he is sad at suffering." Resorting once more to vulgarities, she went on to say, "All those religious people who try to act good and tell me to rejoice in my suffering will just burn in hell."

Listening to Leslie, I was overwhelmed by the incredible mystery and paradox of God's grace. Leslie was deeply troubled. Leslie's life seemed seriously fouled up, although she used a different word for it. Leslie was from a different world than my own, and perhaps from your own; perhaps a different "tribe," perhaps almost a different "race." But Leslie threw herself entirely on God's mercy and grace, in desperation and pain. I could picture the Samaritan woman encountering Jesus, that man from another tribe, at the well in John chapter four. I could picture the adulteress, brought to Jesus by the legalists in John chapter eight. Jesus did not accuse or point his finger at either woman. His response was Good News to them! But his response was a stumbling block to the religious people (I Cor. 1:23). Grace is just not fair.

Now of course we do not sin just so that grace may abound. But the Bible says, "While we were yet sinners, Christ died for us" (Romans 5:8 RSV). The Bible says, "For by grace are ye saved, through faith...not because of works, lest any man should boast" (Ephesians 2:8 RSV). And in case anybody dares to respond that while salvation is by grace, continued growth and holiness is by works, Paul retorts calling the Galatians "idiots" for supposing that we begin in the spirit but end in the flesh (Galatians 3:1 Phillips). He angrily concludes that anyone who insists on the way of doing good works, should be emasculated (Galatians 5:11)! Wouldn't you love to hear Paul and Leslie have a chat? They might just get along!

What paradoxically Good News this message must have been to sinners. What an affront and scandal it must have been to the religious. Grace, especially extended to others, is just not fair. How does it make *you* feel?

Paradox and Liberating Arts...

A friend of mine, Sharon Parks, formerly at the John F. Kennedy School of Government at Harvard, has suggested that true religion is paradoxical. It captures tragedy and hope in one swoop; maybe a little like the dissonance of blues music or the novels of black women such as Mildred Taylor.

First, faith embraces and sorts out dissonance, using imagination to stand in another's shoes, even a prostitute's shoes, or Leslie's shoes. At the close of a week on racial reconciliation do you exercise imagination to stand in another's shoes? In a place like Greenville, where disagreement is the fuel of discovery, do you push for closure or patiently imagine new approaches?

Second, faith also expands our boundaries, using courage to include those outside our tribe, outside our race, gentiles, Samaritans, even drunken fellow airplane passengers. At the close of a week on racial reconciliation do you exercise courage to expand your boundaries of friendship and acceptance? When you encounter religious and cultural diversity, even here on campus, do you exercise courage to consider alternative ways of thinking or do you hide defensively behind lines drawn in the sand and behind your own way of doing things? Grappling with the paradox of grace requires profound imagination and courage.

So now that I think of it, I suppose in the end this *is* a talk about my philosophy of education. I suppose it *is* about liberal arts as liberating arts. Because it is about Good News that releases captives, gives sight to the blind, and liberty to those who suffer, even to Leslie. The paradox is that liberation can be a stumbling block today even as it was so many years ago.

My Note...

As our plane dropped into St. Louis last Friday night, I handed Leslie the note I had promised her and I asked her not to read it until she was at home; and sober I hoped. It said:

> Dear Leslie,
> You wanted me to write you a note. Here it is. (Smiley face). I'm so glad you believe the Bible is God's Word and I hope you keep reading it and reading it and reading it. I'm sorry your life has been so full of suffering and that so many of us who say we follow Jesus are such legalists & hypocrites. But I can't agree with you more that Jesus accepts us just where we are and wants us to draw nearer to Him. Leslie, there is nothing you can do to make Him love you any more OR any less than he already does. I stake my life on that. I hope you will see Him more clearly every day.
>
> Jim

I don't know what will happen to Leslie. She is struggling like the rest of us to embrace the paradox of God's grace.

FOUR

SUFFERING: BAD NEWS FOR GOOD PEOPLE

MAY 4, 1999

Introduction...

This semester I have enjoyed speaking to you twice. Each time I have talked about paradox. The first time I talked about how sometimes we have vision but still cannot see. Then I talked about the paradox of grace which extends good news even to those like Leslie who have struggled.

As I told you last time, you will likely hear me say much about this theme of paradox over the months and years because I believe that learning to grapple with complexity and ambiguity and apparent paradox is perhaps the single most essential element of a liberal arts education.

Today, as I did last time, I wanted to talk to you about my philosophy of education; how growth is all about stretching ourselves intellectually, morally, and spiritually. But that was before I reflected on what the last six weeks have meant. That was before Kosovo, Littleton, and a call from Barnes Hospital.

Events Since March 22...

Kosovo: On March 24, only two days after I spoke to you last time, bombing began over Kosovo. In the few weeks since that time, over 500,000 ethnic Albanians have been thrown out of their homes and country and forced to flee to refugee camps in neighboring states. 750,000 or more are homeless. There are countless dead, including many civilians from NATO airstrikes but also from the genocidal murders uncovered by satellite photographs of mass graves.

The U.S. has already spent $1 billion on this undeclared war and has appropriated a total of $12 billion more. That is enough by itself to feed all the starving people on earth for months or even an entire year. While three American soldiers have been released, the bombing continues, people are dying every day, and with almost daily allusions to Vietnam, we are haunted by the question, "Where will it end?"

Littleton: On April 20, at 11:25 a.m., two young men about your age, with hearts poisoned by anger and self-indulgence, deliberately savaged the place where they were supposed to be learning. It was Hitler's birthday. *Time* magazine, on their front cover, called them the "Monsters Next Door."

And what was perhaps more horrifying than even the murders themselves— if that is possible—was their laughing attitude about it all. Solzhenitsyn suggests in *A Day in the Life of Ivan Denisovich* that the purest form of evil is laughter in the face of suffering.

Among the most sickening accounts of Littleton was that of a young girl interviewed within hours of the shootings describing how she had begged not to be killed, and then watched as her assailant agreed but turned with a laugh to shoot her friend in the face instead.

And we have all now heard of Cassie Bernall. When she was asked by one of the killers, "Do you believe in God?" she paused, and then apparently quite aware of what the consequences might be, is said to have replied, "Yes, I do." Her fellow student turned murderer asked her "Why?" then killed her before she could answer. Last night I did a web search for her name and found twenty-two thousand entries in news groups alone!

Barnes: On April 1, I spent a glorious day at the zoo with my daughter. It was warm and sunny; one of those special father-daughter times. We even slept on the bench in front of the brown bears, her favorites. We were waiting for my wife Ellen to have a routine bone scan as she established new doctors in this new area. Over the next few days, we had a wonderful Easter with our son joining us too.

But after they both had left, on Monday, April 5, Ellen took a call which most of you now know told her that her cancer had returned after eleven years. Yesterday we took another call which set the stage for treatment but left the long-term prognosis very uncertain. So, there were tears in the Mannoia house last night. [Postscript: Ellen fought breast cancer for almost exactly eight more years from the time of this address and died, June 13, 2007.]

Suffering...

In one way or another each of these events since the last time I spoke to you is really about suffering. So, I would like to talk to you today a little about what that means. It is surely a sober and somber topic. And in many ways, it is both *uninteresting* and *difficult*. It is *uninteresting*, at least sometimes for young people, because often you have not experienced it much. Of course, for some of you, that is not at all true. Abuse and prejudice are no respecter of age. But for others, suffering is a stranger. And to hear of the suffering of others hardly makes a dent because young people cannot help seeing themselves as immortal. Bad things—even Littleton—only happen to other people; it could never happen here, to me.

But the subject is also *difficult*. That is because first, the nature of the human spirit is to close out of memory those experiences which have involved suffering. People just don't remember it well. But second, and what is more, even to those for whom it is fresh, suffering is a shocking kind of experience. There is profound initial grief; the kind I have described to friends over the past weeks that makes you want to throw up every moment. You can't believe it is happening to you. But quickly it becomes shock. And shock numbs the experience of suffering into an anesthesia which is dreamlike and unreal.

You don't feel anything at all. Just look at the TV images of refugees streaming from Kosovo and you will see an empty look which explains why it is hard to talk about suffering. So, it is difficult to say much about suffering because one who suffers can hardly know, much less describe, how they feel. I stand before you numb, finding it hard to feel much of anything at all, and so it seems with little to say. But let me try.

Philosophical and Pastoral...

Suffering is a big part of the problem of evil. That is the longstanding problem of how a God who is all powerful and at the same time all loving can allow evil to occur at all. For millennia Christians have struggled to understand this. In addressing the problem one must not fail to distinguish two approaches: the pastoral and the philosophical.

The *pastoral* is supportive, concerned with the heart of the sufferer, while unfortunately, the *philosophical* often seems cold and calculating. But since here at Greenville we are engaged in the life of the mind please understand my intentions. My words are hardly soothing to me or to any others who suffer. What I want to offer you today is not a triumphalist statement of anyone's victory over suffering, but rather a model, or at least a testimony, for embracing that paradox of suffering which makes it a means to share in Christ's suffering and become like him. How can that be?

C.S. Lewis...

According to C. S. Lewis, "God whispers to us in our pleasures, speaks in our conscience, and shouts in our pain...it is His megaphone" (*Problem of Pain*, p. 93). What does this mean?

In the first place, pain shatters our illusion that all is well, taking with it our concept of self-sufficiency. As St. Augustine is said to have put it, "God wants to give us something but our hands are full" (*City of God*). To put it more plainly, the proud are in constant danger of finding the present life so good we do not turn to God. This is especially true for the young and unfortunately, for those in academics.

It is almost an endemic sin that academics, whether faculty or students, suffer from the illusions of self-sufficiency. It is surely very American! But pain shatters self-sufficiency and allows instead only true self-sufficiency... the presence of God in us. But "God in us" is not happiness. Instead, it is character building, shaping us to be what we are designed to be; willfully submissive to our creator and Lord.

In James, chapter one, we read "Count it all joy my brothers, when you meet various trials, for you know that the testing of your faith produces steadfastness. And let steadfastness have its full effect, that you may be perfect and complete, lacking in nothing" (James 1:2 RSV). In a word, suffering is "soul building." It may be joy, but it is not happiness.

But second, there is more to suffering than soul building. There is a mysterious cosmic participation at stake as well. Because the fall has alienated our desire from God's will, the only way to be *sure* we act for God's sake is if we act contrary to our desire; contrary to what we like. The ultimate test or expression of a creature's highest good, her return to God, is obedience born of a will stripped naked of desire.

So, acting out surrender *requires* pain. Only one motive is then possible, surrender to God in us. Then when we do act *from* God in us, prompted by the presence of suffering which authenticates our surrender, we are live instruments of creation, participating with our brother Jesus himself in *undoing* Adam's act. This is why martyrdom, whether that of our great Suffering Servant or our own, is the ultimate Christian act.

Suffering and Education...

We have talked of physical suffering in Kosovo and Littleton. And we have imagined the numbing effects of emotional suffering too. But what of mental suffering? Here, unsurprisingly, my words circle back to the liberal arts. Oswald Chambers says there is always a struggle for self-expression: "Make a practice of provoking your own mind to think out what it accepts easily" (*My Utmost*, 12/15). Our position is not ours till we make it ours by suffering. The struggle is to express your inarticulate feelings. Liberation comes after suffering. That is the reason that suffering, even in the apparently trivial way you may feel you are doing so now during the days of your final examinations, is essential to the liberating arts and to this place.

Paradox...

So, after all this, what is the paradox of suffering? Let me suggest two answers:

First, *suffering is a good but not one to be pursued.* One might suppose that if something is good, it should be sought out and cultivated. But this is not true for suffering. It is a good means but not a good end. What is good is the submission to the will of God, and suffering can help. As Oswald Chambers puts it, "No healthy saint ever chooses suffering; he chooses God's will, as Jesus did, whether it means suffering or not" (*My Utmost*, 8/10). Thank God for a broken heart but don't ask for it (*My Utmost*, 11/1). With this in mind we can avoid the danger that suffering will be for naught. Too often, as Chambers put it, "we sit on the threshold of God's purpose and die away of self-pity," aided by sympathetic friends (11/1). The point is to embrace our suffering though we have not invited it.

That last phrase from Chambers illustrates a second paradox related to suffering. It is the paradox that, *sympathy—our response to suffering in others—is a good to be offered but not a good to be received.* It is dangerous to those who suffer because it can engender self-pity. As C.S. Lewis puts it, "Indignation at others' sufferings, though a generous passion, needs to be well managed lest it steal away patience and humility from those who suffer, and plant anger and cynicism in their stead" (*Problem of Pain*, p. 108). Chambers argues the same principle,

> No saint dare interfere with the discipline of suffering in another saint.... The people who do us good are not those who sympathize with us, they always hinder, because sympathy enervates.... Jesus said self-pity was of the devil (Matthew *16:23*) (*My Utmost*, 8/10).

This sounds altogether cold and ungracious. How can the tender sympathies of friends be dangerous? I have felt the kindness of such sympathy deeply over the past weeks. Remember, the danger here is not for the one who offers it, but for the one who may allow it to detract from the work suffering must do in his heart. That is the work I want for myself and should you suffer, the work I would pray for you too.

Bernall's Poem...

With all this talk of suffering, perhaps little has been said. So, let me finish by taking us back to Cassie Bernall, perhaps—just perhaps—a seventeen-year-old Littleton martyr. According to the *Boston Globe* (April 24, 1999), on the night of her death, Cassie's brother Chris found a poem Cassie had written just two days prior to her death. It read:

> *Now I have given up on everything else*
> *I have found it to be the only way*
> *To really know Christ...and to find*
> *Out what it means to suffer and to*
> *Die with him. So, whatever it takes*
> *I will be one who lives in the fresh*
> *Newness of life of those who are*
> *Alive from the dead.*

FIVE

STRENGTHS: MOSES, DAVID, PETER, AND MY DAD

For the past nine months Greenville College has been talking a lot about "strengths." Last fall, for the first time, all of you freshmen were invited to take a test created by the *Gallup Organization* which seeks to find out what special abilities each of you has. Unlike some of the other popular personality tests, it was developed by empirical research asking hundreds of successful people questions of many many kinds. From their answers, patterns emerged which seem to tell us what answers are given by people who already demonstrate strengths. Then last fall, the *Foundation for Improvement of Post-Secondary Education* gave us hundreds of thousands of dollars to see if we can use this tool to do a better job of matching you to your major and even your choice of initial career by paying attention to those strengths. Greenville is one of only two or three institutions in the country implementing this tool campus wide. The theme of strengths is one which most certainly fits with our college mission to transform each of you for lives of character and service. This is because there can be no better way to help you develop than by recognizing and building on the strengths you already have. But this effort also certainly fits the mission of Christ's church worldwide because the Bible tells us the Church is to be modeled after the Body of Christ. And like any "body," its ability to function depends on each part doing what it does best, working cooperatively, held together by a spirit of common purpose, guided by its head. So, for Greenville College to help you find your strengths will "grow you" individually, but will also build the Body of Christ.

When I took the *Strengths Finder* last fall, I was told my top strengths are, *communication, strategic thinking, ideation, self-assurance,* and *command.* Freshmen, I hope you remember yours! Along with this report came two lessons which have helped me, and I would like to share them with you.

First, I was told that sometimes people make fun of our strengths and it cripples us into thinking we are inadequate. I understand that well from personal experience. Maybe you have felt this too. For example, as a young man I always felt pleased to be able to command, take charge and give direction. It seemed natural. But then for many years my surrounding culture, especially Christian culture taught me this behavior was arrogant, even sinful. Good people were servants and somehow you could not serve if you commanded. After a number of years of serious self-doubt, and conflicted feelings, I came to understand it is okay to be who God made us to be, so long as our heart is right. Motives and character count. So, we must all beware of those who would turn our strengths against us, crippling those strengths by forcing them into reclusion or inactivity.

But we must also beware of our strengths themselves. For paradoxically, our greatest strengths can also be our greatest weaknesses. This second lesson, this paradox of strengths, is the lesson I want you to think about with me for a few minutes.

The night before last I witnessed firsthand what happens when a body becomes divided against itself. When our strength can paradoxically become a weakness. My father was seventy-eight years old. For all those years, the parts of his body had mostly worked together. Of course, there were the obvious exceptions; for example, at times in 1944 when lack of coordination on the GC basketball court moved his arms one way when the ball needed to go another. But beginning two years ago, the cancer that began to grow in his body, gradually turned his own cells against him. By Sunday (seventy-two hours ago), cells were no longer cooperating, no longer taking "orders" from the brain, or even following the genetic instructions which for all those years had guided the duplication of cells in appropriate places and appropriate numbers. The genetic "scripture" had been violated and the coordinating "head" was being disregarded. The result was the uncontrolled duplication of cells in his chest—tumor growth—which in turn selfishly drew fluids from every other part of his body, failing to allow those fluid cells to do their work in other places. While those fluids would normally provide added resources in times of trouble, a strength to combat disease or weakness, under these circumstances, in the presence of the outbreak of biological civil war, the strength itself became a weakness. The accumulated fluids filled his chest, reducing his ability to provide fresh oxygen to his body elsewhere. In response, his brain called on his heart to do more and more and more, pumping faster and faster to push more blood through the restricted lungs, snatching what oxygen was available. By Sunday night, his pulse was at 150, not much for a young athlete, but for someone his age, it was a taxing workout, that went on hour after hour all through the night and into the next day. It was by comparison as if one of you ran full speed all day and all night without stopping. His heart never failed him. But the lack of oxygen exchange meant blood "cargo cars" ran empty to the brain, and eventually shut down the very brain sending those desperate messages for help to the loyal hardworking heart. Then Monday night at 11:27 p.m., my father died, a victim of fluid friends turned enemies, his own cells in rebellion, a strength turned against himself. He was a man of God, a Greenville alum, and my greatest earthly inspiration of what it means to be a man of character and service.

I think there is a lifetime of sermons buried in that story; or maybe they just jump out at me because I need their lessons so much. The heart needs the head as much as the head needs the heart. Our lives must be ordered by the design structured in our creation. Whether genetic DNA or biblical truth, if we disregard that code of life, we risk the biological or spiritual civil war that destroys us from the inside out. But the one I want to underscore, is the paradox that our strengths may be our weaknesses. Put in a nutshell, my point to you today is never to forget that our strengths and our weaknesses are often flip sides of the same coin.

Let me try to illustrate in another way. I have already said one of my strengths is command. I am told it is useful to have someone with this strength around in a time of crisis. But the "flip side" is that often such decisiveness becomes abruptness and insensitivity to others. I see it hurt other people and I am sorry. I'm also told one of my strengths is communication. But the "flip side" of that is that I'm aware that often I don't listen well enough. Unfortunately, I could go on. The irony then is that precisely the things which we have to contribute to others can end up becoming our weaknesses and rendering our efforts less effective and even harmful.

The Bible is full of examples. In the words of Oswald Chambers, in *My Utmost for His Highest* (4/19) *"The Bible characters fell on their strong points, never their weak ones."* Several cases come to mind, and I am sure you could easily add to the list.

Take Moses. His sense of justice was clearly a strength. He was outraged at the way his people were treated by the Egyptians. Unfortunately, this strength led to his murder of the Egyptian taskmaster. Fortunately, this strength also drove the passion of his defiance of the Pharaoh, leading eventually to his leadership of the exodus of his people into liberty. But in the end, this same strength, this passion for justice, drove him to anger with the people at Meribah, an anger that overrode his willingness to listen to the Lord's instructions, prompted him to take matters into his own hands, and in his disobedience denied him access ultimately even to the promised land itself.

Or take David. Here was a man of action. His strength was his "can do attitude." What else prompts a young boy to stand up to a lion, a bear, and even a giant when others shrink back in fear? No theorizing here. No committee work needed. Just the bottom line please. Yet when his passion for Bathsheba surfaced, his "can do" attitude convinced him he "could do" with her whatever he wanted, and the consequence was murder and adultery.

Or what about Peter. Peter's strength was his courage. This man was simply unafraid. What else prompts someone to leap from a boat to walk on water? What else makes a lifetime Jew even consider eating what was unclean, associating with gentiles, and thereby encouraging Paul's ministry? That ministry and the teachings of salvation by grace not works eventually helped us understand how it possible for each one of us to stand in relation to God through Christ. But wasn't it also Peter's lack of fear that made him leap to cut the ear from Caiaphas' servant in the garden of Gethsemane, missing the purposes of his Master? And how ironic that this act arising out of his "strength" led only minutes later to his groveling cowardice in the face of no more than a mere maiden in the High Priest's courtyard. Our strengths not only become our weaknesses, but they turn upon us and become our worst enemies.

Unchecked, and fueled by the cancer of our sinful nature, our strengths turn upon us too, making our lives ones of spiritual civil war.

I wish I could say there is some easy fix to this dilemma. But like most of the paradoxes I've tried to describe to you in chapels over the course of two years, this one too does not submit to easy solutions. I think the tension, the paradox, between recognizing, affirming, and exercising our strengths, while avoiding the dangers they pose, is a tension we must all face every day of our lives. It is in fact the very stuff of life that we must grapple with this dilemma from youth to old age and even to death. As Chambers puts it, *"Unguarded strength is double weakness"* (*My Utmost*, 4/19).

Spring is the season of hope. So, let us remain alert. And most of all, let us remember, *"'Kept by the power of God' that is the only safety"* (*My Utmost*, 4/19, 1 Peter 1:5 KJV).

SIX

TRUST: MISSING MY FLIGHT

DECEMBER 3, 2001

It was Christmas time thirty-two years ago! I finished my packing and dragged my suitcase and the huge box wrapped in rope downstairs. The dorm sat on Memorial Drive which snaked along the Cambridge side of the Charles River across from Boston. The snowy sidewalks made it just a little easier to pull the box and suitcase the long four blocks to the Kendall Street subway station for the noisy ride to Logan Airport. I had worked all summer driving a truck, delivering Hood Milk to all the grocery stores on Cape Cod to earn enough money to buy the cheapest round trip ticket from Boston to São Paulo, Brazil. The awkward box contained a small black and white television my missionary parents had asked me to bring to them since electronics were outrageously expensive down there. I had an international connection to make in Miami, so when my flight left an hour late because of snow, I worried all the way to Florida.

When I emerged in the Miami terminal, I panicked realizing I had only five minutes to get to the gate of APSA, Aerolineas Peruvianas, S.A. I'll never forget running with that huge cardboard box; thoughts of six months of work and planning adding burden to the awful aching of a son who missed his family and only got to see them or even talk to them once a year. It was too late. The agent pointed out the window at the jet which was taxiing away from the gate. I was sick. I stood and watched the plane for almost half an hour, delayed on the runway for unknown reasons, before it eventually raced into the humid night air headed for Brazil with my heart aboard. The agent informed me that a small airline like APSA did not fly daily to Brazil and did not transfer tickets to other airlines that did. So, although they would pay my motel bill, it would be a three-day layover. Without phones, even my telegram didn't get through in time, so my family made a fruitless four-hour journey to the airport only to leave wondering and worried why I didn't get off the plane. My motel room was cheap, and my choice of a newly released novel to read late into the night was not a good one. Under those circumstances, especially at Christmas time, let me suggest you not select the book *Rosemary's Baby*!

During the next intervening day, I walked to a grocery store to buy my mother some lime flavored *Jell-O*, something else unavailable in Brazil. As I walked back to the motel through a residential neighborhood, a police cruiser pulled up, the officer asked me to spread out on the hood of the cruiser and searched me thoroughly. Apparently, the locals thought it was suspicious that a longhaired man should be walking—not driving—through a residential area carrying a brown paper bag. When the officer asked me where I lived, I said I was staying at the Starlight Motel. When he asked why, I said because I was leaving for Brazil the next morning. When he asked what was in the little brown bag, I said lime *Jell-O* for my mother. When he asked for ID, I showed him my student ID from M.I.T. in Boston.

All of these were apparently the wrong answers, particularly because unbeknownst to me there was an "all-points bulletin" out for an M.I.T. technician who had committed murder in Boston that week and fled to Florida! To make a long story short, I spent the rest of the day riding in the back seat of the cruiser, while the officer radioed to check me out. After several hours, and no reply from the FBI in Washington, he let me out at my motel. He cheerfully concluded that he now knew me better than any FBI report, wished me a Merry Christmas, sent greetings to my mom and dad, and hoped I would enjoy the *Jell-O* dessert!

Well, I did make it to Brazil, and spent three glorious weeks in the summer sun and on the Atlantic beaches of Santos. But the return was gruesome. You have to understand that in those days, final exams and the break between fall and spring semester were not right *before* Christmas but *after* Christmas in late January. It was a terrible arrangement! Stretching my visit home as much as possible, I arrived back in Boston tanned, but in a blinding snowstorm, stomach aching to be back with my family, having utterly forgotten whatever little quantum mechanics and numerical analysis I had managed to cram into my brain in the ancient history of the previous long fall. Now I faced two weeks of snowy grey overcast days trying to cram for those exams. My teachers were obviously demon possessed—remember I had just read *Rosemary's Baby*. They were bent people, bound on humiliating me or even breaking me if possible. I was deeply in love with a girlfriend at Wellesley, the Vietnam War raged, the government was about to conduct the infamous draft lottery, and my roommate (later to found and run Grafpoint Software in Silicon Valley) had stayed in the dorm the entire break studying. To understate the point dramatically, Jim Mannoia was not motivated to study for finals!

Maybe you feel a little that way today? Maybe you feel your professors are asking too much—if not demon possessed then at least obsessed? Maybe you are thinking about bigger issues in your life or in your world; that special relationship, the war in Afghanistan, the fear of terrorism, the sagging economy and your bills to pay. Maybe you're wondering why you are in college at all? I think I know how you feel. I've talked with quite a few faculty in the past weeks and some of them report a sense that for some of you motivation may be in short supply. Even Pastor Kay at the Free Methodist church mentioned in a sermon a few weeks ago his surprise that more students weren't "taking notes in class" the day he visited.

I'd like to share the story of a good friend who also struggled with motivation. His struggle came to a climax outdoors one night in a garden in the Kidron Valley, the Garden of Gethsemane. As Jesus faced his final examination before Caiaphas, Pilate, and ultimately on Golgotha, he struggled mightily with motivation.

Now your first reaction may be to object that it is Christmas time and Gethsemane is an Easter story. But the Christmas story is about incarnation and it has two focal points. One was the decision in heaven preceding Jesus' birth and the other the struggle in Gethsemane. Both occasions were unimaginable struggles of motivation precisely because the act of God becoming human is painful. And I mean painful for God Himself. It represents an unbelievable "squeezing" of the infinite into what is finite. We don't have a record of Father and Son debating this painful step before the birth. But fortunately we do have an account of the debate before the "squeezing" painful step of death on the cross. And the motivational struggle is the same. Gethsemane is perhaps the best "inside" account of Christmas we have:

> Then Jesus went with his disciples to a place called Gethsemane, and he said to them, "Sit here while I go over there and pray." [37] He took Peter and the two sons of Zebedee along with him, and he began to be sorrowful and troubled. [38] Then he said to them, "My soul is overwhelmed with sorrow to the point of death. Stay here and keep watch with me." [39] Going a little farther,

he fell with his face to the ground and prayed, "My Father, if it is possible, may this cup [this final exam] be taken from me. Yet not as I will, but as you will." 40Then he returned to his disciples and found them sleeping. "Could you men not keep watch with me for one hour?" he asked Peter. 41 "Watch and pray so that you will not fall into temptation. The spirit is willing, but the body is weak." 42He went away a second time and prayed, "My Father, if it is not possible for this cup [this final exam] to be taken away unless I drink it, may your will be done." 43When he came back, he again found them sleeping, because their eyes were heavy. 44 So he left them and went away once more and prayed the third time, saying the same thing. "My Father, if it is possible, may this cup [this final exam] be taken from me. Yet not as I will, but as you will."45 Then he returned to the disciples and said to them, "Are you still sleeping and resting? Look, the hour is near, and the Son of Man is betrayed into the hands of sinners. 46Rise, let us go! Here comes my betrayer (Matthew 26:36–44, NIV)!

Let's face it. Jesus was depressed. In His own words (v. 38 NIV) he was, "overwhelmed with sorrow to the point of death." I've felt overwhelmed. Have you? Preparing for those exams that January thirty-two years ago, I grew discouraged. I would put my head on my desk in early hours of the morning and just cry. Only a few years ago, in a new and apparently unmanageable job as a new Vice-President at Houghton College, several times I found myself so overwhelmed, I put my head on my desk and simply cried. "It's just too much, Father!" Maybe you've been there? I hugged a College employee who felt that way this week. My son and daughter are there this week with their final exams. My daughter even gave me the idea for this talk. Maybe like Jesus your friends are not helping much either. Maybe they're asleep when you're trying to study, when you're facing the biggest motivational struggles of your year, or perhaps even of your life.

Jesus did two things. And they were apparently paradoxical because they seem to be opposite responses. (You knew there had to be paradox somewhere in my chapel talk today didn't you? Well, here it is!) First, he *persisted*. Gethsemane is an account of Jesus' own persistent effort in the face of his disciples' laziness. Jesus did understand that weakness. He said, "The spirit is willing, but the body is weak" (v. 41 NIV). Boy! Doesn't that ring true? At 2 a.m. the spirit may be motivated but the body is certainly weak. Sometimes we imagine this expression as a warning to avoid the temptations of overeating, of indulging inappropriately in alcohol, drugs, pornography, or maybe just indulging inappropriately in strong language or even just spending money. But it seems to me when Jesus says these words in the context of the supreme motivational struggle of his life, he is acknowledging the fundamental struggle of our human condition. Persistence in doing right is not natural. Jesus persisted in his struggle. Verse forty-two says having seen the weakness of his disciples "he went away a second time and prayed." Then in verse forty-three after returning to find them sleeping a second time, "...he left them and went away once more and prayed the third time." In the face of doubt and lack of motivation Jesus persisted again and again into the night despite the weakness of body and the lack of support from friends.

But second, having done all he could, Jesus *trusted* His Father. Paradoxically, he persisted but then he also "let go." Three times, this account tells us Jesus asked that the struggle might pass, but then he "let go" of it into the hands of his Father. In verse thirty-nine, he says, "My Father, if it is possible, may this cup [this final exam] be taken from me. Yet not as I will, but as you will." In verse forty-two he repeats, "My Father, if it is not possible for this cup [this final exam] to be taken away unless I drink it, may your will be done." And finally, in verse forty-four we are told, "So he left them and went away once more and prayed the third time, saying the same thing." I am convinced the *real* final exam for Jesus was not at the Christmas moment of birth, nor at the Easter moment of death, but at those moments of motivational struggle before each when he persisted but then ultimately relinquished, letting go, trusting His heavenly Father. Can you persist in your hard work far into the night? But then can you let go and say, "Father...not my will but thine be done" (Luke 22:42 KJV)?

There is an old song we sing in the church; "*Trust and Obey, for there's no other way.*" That is the Christmas message I leave with you today, a message of dealing with the struggle for motivation, a message of preparing for final exams. Trust and obey, or perhaps in better order, obey and then trust. Persist and then "let go." The example of our Lord and friend Jesus reminds us that:

> ...[W]e do not have a high priest who cannot sympathize with our weaknesses, but One who has been tempted in all things as we are, yet without sin. [16] Therefore let us draw near with confidence to the throne of grace, that we may receive mercy and may find grace to help in time of need (Hebrews 4:15–16, NASB95).

May the Christmas message, incarnate in the persisting then trusting example of our Lord, help you as you prepare for your final exams.

SEVEN

HOPE I: BERNARDO'S AUNT

JANUARY 30, 2002

In the past two or three months I have been wrestling with another one of those paradoxes you hear me talk of so often. I guess I would call this one the conflict between adopting an attitude of realism and the attitude of hope. It seems I am constantly torn between being realistic and being hopeful. I often just don't know which attitude to take. Let me give you some examples.

Just before Christmas I traveled for four days, visiting friends of the college in Kansas City, Denver, New Jersey, and Manhattan. I flew six legs, on four different airlines, and in ninety-six hours was searched twelve times, finding myself on at least three occasions standing in a crowd in my stocking feet. My nail clipper was "de-filed," meaning the nail file was broken off. And I was the one "randomly chosen" to be "wanded" with the electronic beeping stick; randomly chosen every time it was possible. Early this month I traveled to London with the choir. The same serious security repeated itself. Last weekend I visited three donors in southern California. Having waited on Sunday afternoon for forty-five minutes in a line, my wife and I were rudely told my "personal item" was not a personal item at all and we would have to go through another long wait to check bags before returning to stand again in the same forty-five-minute line. Ellen was angry; I felt humiliated and powerless. Through it all, I struggled to understand the need to be realistic about terrorism and to change the way we do the "travel business" in our country while at the same time hoping it was all going to become less burdensome and humiliating.

For many months I have also been watching the political situation in Zimbabwe. My love for that country comes from the two years my family and I spent there fourteen years ago. With hopes to launch GC's exciting new off-campus program there this fall, I have watched the once stable nation slide into both economic and political turmoil. I follow the news of bad inflation, of new laws to hamper a fair election on March 9, and government supported lawlessness to take property without fair payment. Realistically speaking it has not been a happy few months. Yet I pray harder and harder, hoping for the best, hoping for things to change, and even acting on that hope by signing a lease with an option to buy 300 acres there for a new Greenville "campus."

Elsewhere in the world, events navigate between realism and hope too. Argentina's economy collapses and the effects are felt at the World Bank and around the world. Last year's peace in Northern Ireland teeters in the wake of school shootings. Afghanistan stabilizes, but warlords jockey for power, while nearby Pakistan and India threaten nuclear confrontation. And of course, in the Middle East I cannot imagine how U.S. envoy Zinni knows how to balance realism and hope in the seemingly never-ending negotiations between Israel and the Palestinians.

The challenge comes home too. As the economy here in the U.S. has fluctuated since 9/11, I have imagined the caution and hesitation this can create in the minds of prospective donors to our college, as well as in the minds of prospective students for this spring and next fall. As Enron tumbles into bankruptcy and K-Mart declares Chapter 11, I see evidence our recession is worsening. But then when Greenspan says he will not lower interest rates again, and I hear multiple experts predict an autumn comeback, I see the market move up and I am hopeful the recession has bottomed out. All the while I wrestle with decisions about pricing and enrollment for Greenville College for next fall, along with decisions about the timing of a comprehensive campaign to maintain the wonderful momentum we have felt in recent years on campus. How much does realism impact hope?

Last fall, Ellen needed no chemotherapy, and felt little or no pain. It was a wonderful four months of hope. But just a few minutes from now, she and I will make our pilgrimage to Barnes Hospital to begin the sixth round of chemotherapy in three years. Her pain has returned, and now it's likely her newly regrown hair will soon disappear again. How do we balance realism and hope?

Both realism and hope, it seems, are good things. When realism is neglected hope becomes fantasy and we live in a world of denial. That is true for our response to terrorism in the air, for our decisions about politics in Zimbabwe, for our plans regarding the college, and certainly for my family's plans for life. But when hope is neglected realism becomes resignation and we live in a fatalistic world that paralyzes and robs us of joy. Then our suffering fails to stretch us, and you have heard me speak too many times to forget that I believe stretching is essential for growth.

So, as I prepared to speak with you today, I thought I would remind you of the need to hold these two goods things in tension, to recognize their paradoxical nature, and to embrace this paradox as the high calling of thoughtful mature people. I believe that message is true. But when I began to turn to God's Word, I found a deeper, more profound message. When I searched for passages that called us to realism, I was disappointed. There are not many. Romans 12:3 (NIV) stands out: *"Don't think more highly of yourself than you ought, but rather think of yourself with sober judgment in accordance with the measure of faith God has given you."* That is surely a lesson in realism for those of us who wrestle with pride; something I suppose in one way or another we all do. But when I searched for illustrations of hope, Scripture bubbles up and literally runs over and over and over. Friends, in God's Word, "Hope Wins!"

Of course the message is not that hope prevents suffering; or that hope is fulfilled quickly; or that hope is easy; or even that hope is just a good feeling.

On the contrary, first, hope is usually rooted in suffering. In Romans 5:2–4 (NIV), Paul tells us *"…We rejoice in the hope of the glory of God. Not only so, but we also rejoice in our sufferings, because we know that suffering produces perseverance; perseverance, character; and character, hope."*

Second, hope is patient. The passage I just read says suffering leads to patience as part of the path to hope. Later on, in Romans (8:25 NIV), Paul underscores that hope is patient. *"But if we hope for what we do not yet have, we wait for it patiently."*

Third, hope is hard because it calls us beyond what we see. In the next verse, Paul says, *"For in this hope we were saved. But hope that is seen is no hope at all. Who hopes for what he already has?"*

And finally, hope is more than a feeling; it is an effort of mind. Hebrews 6:12 (NIV) tells us:

> We want each of you to show this same diligence to the very end, so that what you hope for may be fully realized.[12] We do not want you to become lazy, but to imitate those who through faith and patience inherit what has been promised.

And in 1 Peter 1:13 (NLT), we read, "*So prepare your minds for action and exercise self-control. Put all your hope in the gracious salvation that will come to you when Jesus Christ is revealed to the world.*" Even I Thessalonians 5:8 makes the same point symbolizing hope as an armored helmet that protects not our heart but our mind!

I could make the point that "Hope wins" by elaborating each of these four characteristics. But instead let me tell you the story of Bernardo Rodriguez and his aunt. I have learned about him this week in a book I have been reading by Jonathan Kozol (*Amazing Grace*, Jonathan Kozol, Broadway Paperbacks: New York, 1995, Kindle Version). To understand his story well however, I must first tell you a little about where Bernardo lived. South Bronx, just north of downtown Manhattan, the "center" of Western wealth and symbolic of American success, is a tragedy of poverty and suffering. Consider these glimpses.

The 1273 apartments in thirty-eight buildings comprising Diego-Beekman Houses are some of the most physically repelling and profoundly dangerous buildings in America. Between 4000 and 5000 people live here, paying nearly $1000 a month for two-bedroom apartments to a private company in Boston. They are subsidized by the government for all but $200-$250, thirty to forty percent have no telephones, often the ceilings have holes that allow one literally to see into the apartment above, water runs down through the holes when people above attempt to shower, and no more than twelve percent of the residents have jobs. Unemployed adults and youth, often dealing or using drugs, constantly occupy the halls and entries and stairwells. It is not uncommon to see users with rubber ties around their arms and needles sticking in their veins leaning against the entry doors of the building or in the hallways as you go in and out (Kozol, pp. 68ff).

Rats large enough to climb trees and kill squirrels emerge from the river at dusk in hordes, eat through walls, and chew up telephone lines. A Kentucky Fried Chicken and a grocery store were forced to close permanently because the rats were tearing open food boxes. A seven-month-old boy was attacked in his crib three times, and a doctor said it had been years since he had seen bite marks like those on the child's finger. The mother is terrified but can't move out. The city moved her here and she has no money to go anywhere else. The number of rat exterminators has been cut from thirty to ten in a decade, and speaking of doctors, the number available for all NYC schools had dropped from 400 to 23 by the mid-nineties (Kozol, pp. 120,125,128).

The hospitals are frightening places, so ill equipped they sometimes run out of penicillin. A nurse who works in one wears a band stating that in an emergency she is not to be taken there. Referring to Bronx-Lebanon hospital, Mrs. Alice Washington, a resident, reports that whenever her doctor wants to admit her there, she cries. On her last visit, the bed wasn't ready, bloody linen and bandages were everywhere, the toilets didn't work, and she and her family had to clean the room themselves (Kozol pp. 14–15). When this same woman went to the hospital again a few months later, it took from 7 p.m. until 3 a.m. to be admitted, two days to get an X-ray, and she was held for four nights in a basement corridor before a bed was free (Kozol p. 109).

Many of the largely African American residents are either in jail, involved with drugs, or with prostitution. "Rikers Island, a '415 acre Alcatraz in the East River,' was erected largely on compacted trash—less than 1000 yards across the water from the Hunts Point Sewage Treatment Plant" (Kozol, p. 158). The several prisons there house 20,000 inmates, ninety-two percent of them Black and Hispanic. The city spends $58,000/year maintaining each adult prisoner and $70,000/year to maintain each juvenile. In a twelve month period, about 130,000 men and women move in or out of this facility and the others just in South Bronx.

Drug use is everywhere. At one weekly needle exchange in a park, over 1000 addicts are registered. Hundreds arrive each day, turn over their dirty needles and get fresh clean ones. Volunteers and printed materials help them know how to find veins and what to do if they hit an artery. A sign on the walk reports that the park was constructed so that children could be treated with respect! "One young black woman says she uses six needles a day, counts out 60 needles, and is given 60 clean ones for ten days...the whole thing seems almost as normal as a visit to a doctor..." (Kozol pp. 64ff). And of course, there is prostitution:

> The places where you see them most are underneath the Bruckner and the Major Deegan [expressways]. It's dark, but you see them, seven, eight, or nine of them on this side, seven eight, or nine of them on that side. "Some of the women are buck-naked...Even in October, in November." "How much do they make? Three dollars...or five dollars...." "How many are addicted?" "All of them are. You wouldn't do that for three dollars otherwise" (Kozol p. 75).

So that is realism in South Bronx. But where then is the *hope?!*

Let me conclude by sharing Kozol's account of eight-year-old Bernardo Rodriguez, told by his nineteen-year-old aunt, and suggesting how hope wins. Kozol says his interview has "an other-worldly feeling:"

> She begins by telling me that the elevator in the building had been broken for a long time. "Something was wrong with it and people had complained. There had always been some blackish grease that dripped down from the ceiling. My mother had asked the management to fix it, but I don't think anything was done.... The day he died, it was 6:30 in the afternoon...I was sitting with my mother here in the apartment. A neighbor came up and knocked on the door and said, "There something wrong. There's something sticky dripping from the elevator." My mother said, "It's only grease." But the woman said, "It looks

like blood." So then my mother was afraid and went downstairs to check, and it was blood, and it was coming through the ceiling of the elevator, which was [stuck] on the second floor. So then my mother came upstairs to make sure that the children were all right. We found the other children but we could not find Bernardo.... [B]asically, that's when security was called. And then police. They found his body down there on the elevator roof." [While playing in the hall, he leaned against the door, which opened and he fell four stories through the open shaft and struck the elevator roof.... [He] was not discovered until his blood began to drip on passengers. "We couldn't believe it" (Kozol p. 103)!

Kozol continues his interview asking Bernardo's aunt about the little boy, her nephew. She reports he was a good student, loved everyone, said his prayers and had even had his first communion. In the light of such horror, Kozol asks:

How do you handle this? It seems as if it ought to be unbearable. How do you remain so calm? What gives you strength? "I pray [she said]." Does praying really ease the pain? "Yes, it does.... If God has taken him, I know it must be for a reason. He must have needed him in heaven. He must have wanted him. He must have said, 'This boy is better off with me in my own kingdom.'"

The mystery, Kozol wondered, was how Bernardo's aunt could possibly accept such a hopeless, apparently pointless death. She answers in an apparently paradoxical way:

"In a way I don't accept," she answers finally, "and in another way I do...." "God knows when somebody has suffered long enough. When it is enough, he takes us to His kingdom" (Kozol pp. 115ff).

Kozol finishes his story:

In the hallway I notice the elevator door still seems quite loose, and although it doesn't open when I press it, I decide to walk down to the street. The stairway smells and its walls are smeared with something greenish (Kozol pp. 115ff).

So, there we see *realism* and there we see *hope*. Which do you choose?

EIGHT

PEACE: POLITICS AND PLAYGROUNDS

MAY 6, 2002

Last Tuesday night a tragic duet was heard around the world. I listened as CNN and other news agencies carried live audio feeds of automatic weapon fire sounding against the background of church bells tolling in Manger Square in the town of Bethlehem. For over a month now, 200 Palestinians have been barricaded inside the Church of the Nativity, traditionally taken to be the birthplace of Jesus. That night the "Battle of Bethlehem" intensified. Fires broke out, damaging the structure and killing at least one of those in the church. The standoff has become a flash point in the latest round of vicious hostilities between Jews and Palestinians. Yasser Arafat is said to be personally "controlling" the Palestinians in the church, forty of whom are said to be "senior terrorists" wanted by the Israeli government. He claims Israelis are using the standoff as a way to make Palestinians appear disrespectful of Christian traditions, thereby adding to the suspicion and hostility Christians have already toward Muslim believers since 9/11 [September 11, 2001, attack on the World Trade Center in New York]. But Israelis claim the fires and explosions were set by Palestinians to make the Israelis seem the aggressors and seem disrespectful of Christianity, even showing video with glass exploding outward as evidence the source was internal to the church. Both sides are posturing for the North American audience. Watching the orange flames shoot from the church, and listening to the outrageously dissonant sounds, I grew cynical reflecting on the hatred that has fueled this conflict for thousands of years! This will never end. After agreements and summits and promises for as long as I can remember, nothing changes. There's nothing to be done. Leave them to their hatred and killing. It's impossible. The hostile sounds I heard in that duet, echoed ironically against the harmonious memory of the Christmas carol: "O little town of Bethlehem, how still we see thee lie!" and "Silent Night, Holy Night, All is calm, All is bright...Sleep in perfect peace, Sleep in perfect peace." Peace I thought to myself, can never come.

That evening, I felt I wanted or needed to say something to you today about peace. Though it wasn't clear at the time, seemed remarkably less clear last night at midnight, and is only somewhat clearer today, it seemed to me that there may be a few among you who at this time of the semester or at this season of your life, don't have much peace. My mind went especially to you seniors. It is a difficult time of your life. All week I've thought about you. One of you even prayed in morning worship yesterday, "Lord, give seniors a sense of peace in this difficult time, facing their future." You may be preoccupied with so many things that they disrupt your relationships, distracting you and burdening you. But I have a confession to make. As I struggled to prepare to speak to you about peace, I realized I didn't have much peace myself. I have been concerned about the college, concerned about my children, concerned about my wife, finding it difficult to enjoy the peace I know God promises to us all. Sometimes I think God calls me to speak, and especially to preach, mostly because he has something he needs to teach me. And he knows I won't sit still long enough to listen unless I have to prepare. It seems I myself may be among those most in need of hearing this message. So, I want to talk to you today about peace. And as you might expect, it has a lot to do with character. Will you bow your heads and pray with me?

> May the words of my mouth and the meditation of our hearts be acceptable in your sight O Lord, our strength and our redeemer.

Character & Virtue...

We talk about character a lot at Greenville. We expect you to become people of character. With God's help, that's our mission. But after all, what is character anyway? After decades living with me, now every time I point out to my daughter that the stretching challenges she is facing at the moment are "good for her character," she's quick to reply, "Thank you very much, Dad, but I think I have quite enough character already!" Until it got too corny, I used to reply, "Well there's no doubt you're quite a character." But most of us recognize that *character* refers to the deepest fiber of our identity. In one sense the word could be used to describe just the set of personality traits that distinguish us from one another; the *characteristics* of our personality. More importantly however, I think it means the "backbone"—or lack thereof—that holds all our personal characteristics and quirks together. And like a backbone, it has a number of elements or components. Some of these we call virtues, and some we call vices. Either way, they are the principles at the root of who we are that provide the skeletal structure for our identity. Though they are qualities of who we *are*, in turn they serve as the most important forces that shape our behavior, i.e., what we *do*. In other words, while we may have virtues or vices without acting from them at all, they are most easily known by what they produce. They are "the tendencies in us to behave either for good or for bad."

This close connection between virtues and behaviors, explains why at least since Aristotle, people have believed that the best way to build character, to cultivate virtues, is by practice. Aristotle says that by repeated action, we form habits, the very tendencies to behave, the virtues, that comprise our character. In other words, *behavior shapes character*. For example, as C.S. Lewis put it, if you love others often enough, you will become a loving person. But since the virtues are themselves tendencies to behave, clearly having a certain *character also shapes behavior*. If you are a loving person, you will tend to act in loving ways towards others. Of course, the same is true for the opposing vice of hatred too, as it is for the other virtues and vices of integrity, wisdom, self-discipline, anger, selfishness, and so on. Act selfishly and you become selfish. Become selfish and you will act selfishly. It is a crucial cycle of reinforcement that is at once both obvious and profound. In other words, *we are what we do*, and *we do what we are*.

Usually when we are young, we are not particularly aware of which virtues and which vices we have. That's partly because they are not yet well developed and partly because we are not particularly self-aware. But as time goes on, we begin to see ourselves more clearly. Our actions make our virtues plain—both to others and to us ourselves. Keep watching yourself, as objectively as you can, and you learn a lot about your character.

Until the last fifty years or so there has actually been pretty good consensus on what those virtues should be. Plato argued that there were four cardinal virtues: Wisdom, Courage, Self-discipline, and Justice. By the middle ages, the church had added what they called the three Theological virtues: Faith, Hope, and Love. Today, in our postmodern world, it seems that the very notion of character virtues has disappeared. That's because the very idea of good has disappeared except as a generalization about what people in general or some group in particular happens to choose to believe. Virtue then is made relative to the individual or the group they choose.

Peace...

But what does any of this talk about virtues have to do with peace? Well bear with me and consider first what peace means and how it comes about. It's tempting to suppose that "peace" is a state of external affairs; a state of affairs characterized by the lack of conflict in outward actions and events. There is no peace in the Middle East because there is open conflict, there is shooting, there are suicide bombers destroying innocent lives, there are tanks rolling in the streets of Bethlehem. There is no peace in Afghanistan and Pakistan because American troops are still pursuing Al Qaeda and Taliban. But if peace is merely the lack of open outward conflict, then for the most part all of us should be at peace because most of us are not involved today in open conflict. Yet the tensions and anxieties, the fears, and hostilities we feel suggest we are not at peace. So, peace must be something more.

Seventeen hundred years ago, St. Augustine attempted to clarify this notion of peace from a Christian point of view. Peace, he said, is not just the lack of external conflict, it is the presence of right relationships. Augustine made it clear that it is the well-ordered relationships of each part of our self that makes for peace. Peace of the body, peace of the rational and irrational soul, peace of body with soul, as well as peace between man and man.... "The peace of all things is the tranquility of order. [And] order is the distribution which allots things...each to its own place." (City of God, XIX.13) But Augustine concludes ultimately, that because we are fallen, peace comes only as we subordinate all other relations to that of right relationship between mortal man and immortal God.

Trust...

How do these right relationships of peace come about? Plato had argued that when each part of our self was in right relation to each other part, when each class of society was in right relationship with each other class, the result (he called it Justice not peace) arose from intensive *knowledge training*. But Augustine's key to peace, through right relationship between God and man, came from quite a different source. According to Augustine, right relationships could come only from trust. When the central right relationship is between two persons, it must be a matter of trust, not knowledge. Christians have long concluded that true peace begins not with *knowledge training* but with *trust training*.

But here finally, is where the connection of peace to character emerges. Peace depends on trust, but trust is a virtue of character. Ultimately, Augustine is telling us that real peace, right relationships in family, friendships, society, depend on our cultivation of trust in God. And like all virtues, it comes from practice.

If right relations in the Middle East depend on trust, then there's little wonder there is no peace there. Ariel Sharon and Yasser Arafat have distrusted each other from at least as far back as the 1967 war when they fought each other. Trust is missing. At one time I hoped such trust might exist. I remember the National Prayer Breakfast just a few years ago where I watched Arafat embrace Leah Rabin, widow of the assassinated Prime Minister of Israel with whom Arafat had won the Nobel prize for peace in 1994. It seemed there was trust in that embrace. Arafat also shared that peace prize with Shimon Peres, the man who served then, and ironically also serves now, as Foreign Minister. Was there trust then but not now? Or had there never been real trust there at all?

There are people on this campus who do not trust one another; people you do not trust, people I do not trust; people who do not trust you and do not trust me. More importantly, we often do not really trust God. No wonder we often lack peace.

Trust training comes hard. Over twenty years ago my son Jim and I walked across the street to the playground in our beach town of southern California. He was five or six years old. We'd been there many times before, and most times I had coaxed him onto the swings and climbing platform but had never succeeded in persuading him to slide down the ten-foot fireman's pole. Many times, I had tried, and each time before, I could see the fear in his eyes and could sense his distrust that he would really be okay. Was my son really such a wimp? I remember the struggle in my mind vacillating between my impatience with his apparent fear and my recognition that pressing him too hard would only make matters worse. Could I really be patient? Each time before, he had backed down and we had left with tension, not the peace of right relationship between us. You see, I couldn't reach all the way up to where he had to swing out off the platform and grab the pole. For a moment he would be on his own. You could see that he knew that, so the real issue was whether he believed I could or would catch him if things went wrong. It seemed like hours, though I suspect it was only minutes. He'd lean out, then back off, lean out, then back off again. I knew that if he stepped out once, it would be easier to trust me and to trust himself the next time and the next time and the next time. But pressure and impatience would backfire and make trusting again later all that much harder. It became clear, that trust is a very difficult virtue to build and a very very easy thing to destroy. It depended as much on my trustworthiness as it did on his decision to step out. Trust comes hard. I remember the moment that day when he finally reached out, stepped off the platform letting go of his security and slid down into my arms. His trust produced such joy, such relationship, such peace between us.

Don Richardson, in his book *Peace Child*, tells how as a missionary, he had sought to coax the Sawi headhunters of New Guinea to trust Jesus. Their culture was based on distrust. It was expected that people would deliberately build friendship relationships based on deceit in order eventually to betray one another in war. And the regular wars between villages brought tragedy and disaster to these simple people. There was no peace, either in external events or in internal relationships among the people. Richardson sought to tell them the gospel of Jesus Christ. But in such a climate of distrust, the Sawi couldn't understand. Hearing the story of Jesus' death, they saw Judas Iscariot as the hero. He had cultivated a relationship with Jesus in order to betray him for personal profit. By their standards, he was brilliant, and Jesus was the chump. How would it be possible to teach these people about trust? And without trust, how could they ever know peace? The breakthrough came after many years when Richardson learned of an unusual custom. At rare times, the chief of the village really wishing to make peace, would offer his own son, a tiny baby, who would from that time forward be raised by their enemies. It was the ultimate sacrifice of a people who sought real peace. The child would be raised in the other village, and right relationships could exist because the enemies could trust a chief who had shown himself trustworthy by such an expression of sacrifice. Trust comes hard. When Richardson described the initiative of God the Father in offering his son as a tiny peace child, the Sawi understood that this God could be trusted. Then peace came to their lives not only by cessation of conflict between them, and by right relationships among them, but most importantly by right relationship between them and their Father in heaven.

Trust training, the cultivation of the virtue of trust, requires then an act of our minds in response to the evidence of a trustworthy object for our trust. It doesn't matter whether it is a trustworthy earthly father waiting patiently for his son to choose to trust him, or a Sawi chief waiting for an enemy village to respond in trust to his sacrifice. It doesn't matter whether it is an Israeli or Palestinian negotiator acting to trust or waiting to be trusted, or our trustworthy Heavenly Father, waiting patiently for us His children to choose to respond to him with trust. The message is always the same. Peace comes only by trust, and trust comes only by the risky mental act of the one who wishes to trust, in response to the one who is Trustworthy.

In John 14:27, Christ promised to give us peace, "*Peace I leave with you; my peace I give you. I do not give to you as the world gives. Do not let your hearts be troubled and do not be afraid*" (NIV). But His peace comes only by the act of trusting in Him.

Is there conflict in your mind today? Does that conflict constitute a profound lack of peace? Are you worried about tomorrow? About examinations? About a job for the summer or as a senior, about what's next for the fall? Do you want peace? Peace is right relationship, and that ultimately comes down to right relationship with God. But peace depends on that character virtue of trust.

Listen to the wonderful assurance of this linkage found in Isaiah 26:3 (NIV), "*[God] will keep in perfect peace those whose minds are steadfast, because they trust in* [Him]." Are you at peace? Right relationship with your friends, your family, your Maker? If not, is your mind steadfast in trusting? Or are you vacillating in the emotions of fear and distrust, hesitant to step out until it feels right?

As Oswald Chambers asks:

> Is your mind stayed on God or is it starved? Starvation of the mind, caused by neglect, is one of the chief sources of exhaustion and weakness in a servant's life. If you have never used your mind to place yourself before God, begin to do it now. There is no reason to wait for God to come to you. You must turn your thoughts and your eyes away from the face of idols and look to Him and be saved. Your mind is the greatest gift God has given you and it ought to be devoted entirely to Him (*My Utmost*, 2/11).

Friends, and I speak to myself now too, whether it is for peace with friends, with family, or with God, it will take deliberate acts of trust training. Choose to step out and trust. The reward is a peace that passes understanding!

> Do not be anxious about anything, but in everything, by prayer and petition, with thanksgiving, present your requests to God. [7]And the peace of God, which transcends all understanding, will guard your hearts and your minds in Christ Jesus. (Philippians 4:6–7, NIV).

Sing: *When Peace Like a River*

NINE

DISCIPLINE AND GRACE: WHY IT'S A GOOD IDEA TO WEAR YOUR SEATBELT

I'd like to talk to you today about character. Surprise! Surprise! And in particular, I'd like to talk about two specific virtues of character: Discipline and Grace, and how they stand together in a relation that is paradoxical. Surprise again right?! In fairness, I should point out that when Dan and Nick called me last Thursday night on their WGRN nighttime program "Vision" they broadcast my request for topics for me to address today in chapel—but no one called in. So sorry! You get character and paradox again!

Before I go any farther however, I hope you won't mind if I say just a word about this little joke we share about my obsession with character and paradox. Let's just say, hypothetically of course, that someone actually asked you next month, or say on April 1, 2020, what you remember about chapel at Greenville College, and particularly about what that president—"What was his name?"—talked about. You might actually remember "character and paradox;" but forget what it had to do with anything. So, to save you *and* me some embarrassment, let me offer this answer. You could say something like this:

> Well, this guy always said that *character* was crucial because God cares at least as much about who you become inside as he cares about what you're doing on the outside. Who we are inside, where no one else can see, is our character; made up of many virtues and vices. And he made a big fuss about *paradox* because a good liberal arts education teaches that there are many sides to most issues—including virtues and vices—that are often apparently contradictory. But usually each has an element of truth that deserves our attention and even embrace.

And if you said anything like this, well, let's say I would be absolutely thrilled!

There's a special reason however for picking these two particular virtues today. I pick *discipline* because it's exam time and for most of you, that is the virtue in which most of you stand in the greatest need these coming days. And I pick *grace* because the Christmas season is above all, a season about God's amazing grace in sending His only Son to earth on our behalf. He did it "while we were yet sinners" and deserved only judgment and eternal condemnation. It is thus, the season of discipline and grace. Since discipline usually means following a set of rules or laws, you could say that my comments today are about the paradox of law and grace; or as a subtitle, "Why It's a Good Idea to Wear Your Seatbelt."

Let us pray:

> May the words of my mouth and the meditations of our hearts be acceptable in thy sight, oh Lord, our strength and our redeemer.

Discipline...

I hate it when anyone tells me what to do! Maybe it's genetic; being Sicilian. Even my mom tells a story—though I can't vouch for it—that one day in church at age four, while she was playing the organ and couldn't reach me, I was stomping up and down the front pew in hard shoes, distracting everyone else. When she returned to her seat she immediately and sternly told me to "Sit down!" To this, after complying, I am told I replied, "Well I may be sitting down on the outside but I'm still standing up on the inside!" Or maybe my attitude comes as a holdover from college years during the late 1960s. We used to see a lot of bumper stickers saying, "Challenge Authority" and though I was hardly a pot smoking, rebellious hippie, I was a longhaired independent thinker and figured I could "do it my way." The way to deal with "Monday Monday" was to take the "Bridge Over Troubled Waters," and "All You Needed Is Love." When I began to study philosophy, I realized that I placed a high value on "freedom" even though I also kept a high regard for authority. I was and still am inclined to libertarian philosophy and Arminian theology. I still don't like being told what to do. My wife Ellen will confirm the surest way to get me to turn right when we're lost is to *tell* me I *must* go left! And I confess the Vice-Presidents here know it's not a good idea to tell me there is only one way to do something.

According to Stephen Carter, an African American professor of law at Yale who is very interested in character, we are all "bundles of needs and desires" and we live in a culture that knows nothing about delayed gratification. We want everything our way NOW! Pizza, car rentals, telephone service, instant messaging, exam results, food refills in the DC, sexual gratification, even college degrees and high paying jobs. We are a culture of instant, *not* delayed, gratification. But discipline instead tells us to work and wait, and this flies in the face of instant gratification.

Consider for example three different kinds of disciplines (or laws or rules). First, I hate even laws, rules, or restraints I impose on myself. After twenty-seven years, I still hate the fact I've told myself I'll get up earlier three days a week to exercise. I'm trying to drink more water—and I hate it. Saturday, I wanted to go look at new cars, but told myself that first I had to work on what I was going to say to you today. In short, I hate laws, rules, or disciplines, that force me to do what I don't really feel like doing—even if I'm the one making the rules. And I know many of you feel the same way. This week I was talking with a male student friend about the sexual pressures that arise because young people are ready for sexual activity sometimes by age twelve or thirteen, but college culture discourages marriage until twenty-two to twenty-three or for grad students sometimes even until twenty-six to thirty or more. This means for Christian young people who believe sexual intercourse should be reserved for marriage, there is this terrible period of ten to fifteen years of incredible stress. The demands on self-restraint are excruciating, in a culture of self-indulgent *unrestraint.*

But then there are disciplines imposed from outside too. As part of living with others we agree to disciplines, that we might not otherwise choose to impose on ourselves. We submit to speed limits, stop signs, income taxes, exam schedules, keeping appointments, term paper deadlines, rules about not drinking alcohol or visiting rooms of persons of the opposite sex at certain hours. We agree to submit but we don't like these disciplines either! They are not self-gratifying; they are hard, and we sometimes wonder why we allow these disciplines into our lives.

Then finally, there are disciplines that come for Christians because we submit to the Word of God. These now carry not just the weight of our self-discipline, or even just the community consensus, but the force of God's own expectations for His children. At Greenville College, we believe he calls us to the disciplines of putting others first, peacemaking, self-sacrifice, kindness, honesty, refraining from gossip, from a spirit of criticism, from sexual intercourse outside marriage, and from homosexual behavior of any kind. These disciplines too are usually not self-gratifying and likewise require great self-restraint. When, for example, others around us enter into criticism—whether justified or not—it is easy to join in and allow it to become destructive of others and especially of our own character.

So, what's the point? Well as you know, these forms of self-restraint promote the growth of the character virtue of discipline. And practice is the key. The more we learn to delay gratification in important parts of our lives, the easier it becomes. By this practice, we will have grown the character virtue of discipline. Aristotle said the growth of character is all about forming habits. Oswald Chambers says character formation is all about how we handle the drudgery of life. You know, the hard stuff during exam times! Quoting 2 Peter 1:4–5, Chambers says it is all about "adding character to faith:"

> Drudgery is one of the finest tests to determine the genuineness of our character. Drudgery is work that is far removed from anything we think of as ideal work. It is the utterly hard, menial, tiresome, and dirty work. And when we experience it, our spirituality is instantly tested and we will know whether or not we are spiritually genuine (My Utmost, 2/19).

> No one is born either naturally or supernaturally with character; it must be developed. Nor are we born with habits—we have to form godly habits on the basis of the new life God has placed within us. ...Drudgery is the test of genuine character. The greatest hindrance in our spiritual life is that we will only look for big things to do.... I must realize that my obedience even in the

smallest detail of life has all of the omnipotent power of
the grace of God behind it (*My Utmost, 6/16*).

Dallas Willard, a friend of mine who has written a book about spiritual disciplines, says, the disciplines are like what a baseball player or a musician does if they hope to perform well in their big moments. They practice constantly. The disciplines are not themselves a means of baseball or musical success nor much less by extension, spiritual salvation. But they put us in a condition that allows God to do what he wants to do in shaping who we are becoming.

You might suppose discipline is good because of what it helps you accomplish. While that's partly true, the most important point is that to be a disciplined person is a virtue in and of itself. I believe discipline is a virtue because of what it shows about who you are inside.

In other words, whether in matters of your citizenship, your studies, your sexuality, or your spiritual growth, discipline is a virtue of character.

Grace...

That brings me to the second virtue I want to talk about today; grace. The virtue of grace makes allowances for others; especially when they don't deserve any allowances. It is "unmerited favor." It's returning road rage with kindness. It's being civil even with phone solicitors and other annoying people—for *your* sake as much as for theirs! It's telling the truth about others even when they lie about you.

When our character embodies grace we do not keep accounts of who owes whom what. Grace is not a particular position or opinion. It is a quality of attitude, of heart. This virtue of grace shows itself by the spirit with which we relate to others. Do we think more highly of others than ourselves? Do we consider that someone else's opinion may be worth hearing, not just because it's the polite thing to do, or even because it's the best way to force them to hear ours, but because we recognize their value, and do not need to control or win at every turn?

Gracious people are wonderful to be around. They make space for others. They are not however, merely people pleasers. They typically can let attention focus on someone else not because they are uninteresting or shallow themselves, but often on the contrary because they have enough self-assurance not to need to dominate or control. When you've spent time with gracious people you come away feeling you are the most important person in the world.

Sometimes grace however is confused with mere tolerance. Some people simply don't care what others do or say. This is not grace but just indiscriminate permissiveness; "anything goes." Some even feign graciousness posing behind a façade of pseudosophistication that is deeply arrogant and judgmental. Gracious people have firm convictions, and deep passions. But they hold their views with an openhanded humility that is not easily threatened and seeks improvement.

God was gracious in sending Christ to sacrifice his own life for ungrateful, arrogant creatures. Christ was gracious in seeing the best in each of us, and especially in his weak disciples. His grace allowed—and allows—Him to see through the false pretenses of our weaknesses, our insecurities, and perhaps especially our own self-deceptions. If we do not believe others need grace in dealing with us, then we obviously have not seen ourselves very well. He rises above it all but never with judgment that demeans or belittles. We come from encounters with Christ feeling like the most important person in the world.

Summary...

So, what does the virtue of grace—captured in the spirit of Christmas—have to do with the virtue of discipline? They seem worlds apart; almost contradictory—should I say "paradoxical?" Discipline seems to be all about following rules, those of the community, or the state, or even ones we set for ourselves. But isn't that all really "Old Testament" stuff? Aren't we today "New Testament" Christians, saved by grace and no longer under the law? Shouldn't we "go easy on ourselves," "make room for everyone," tolerate anything, avoid discrimination, include everyone? What's the point of attention to rules and law, of personal discipline, of self-restraint?

A week ago last night, my wife Ellen and I jumped in the car and headed into St. Louis as we have done dozens and dozens of times. We were headed to dinner with a college trustee and her husband who have become good friends. I remarked to Ellen as we pulled away from the stop sign by the "Simple Room" what a wonderful treat it was to have a job that let us travel together on a pleasant Sunday evening in a comfortable car enjoying one another's company for a restful trip to spend the evening with good friends we love and respect deeply. God was good. Sixty seconds later, as I approached the second sweeping left turn headed for Interstate 70 on "Moo Cow Mountain Road," I saw headlights from the other direction coming too fast and at the wrong angle. Seconds later I remember the unforgettable sight of those two headlights twenty feet directly ahead, knowing there was nothing more I could do. The next instant, we plowed head-on into the oncoming car at a combined speed of perhaps more than 110 mph. It was over that fast. I remember thinking, "That was quick!" I remember wondering, "Why didn't the airbags deploy?" then looking down in the darkness to see they had deployed. I asked Ellen if she was all right, and heard her say, "I think so," which relieved my heart. I remember saying I need to get help and looking for my cell phone. I saw it glowing on the floor. I remember hearing a terrible deathly moaning from the other car and a second voice crying out, "Someone please help me get out of here!" As I opened the door while talking to the 911 operator, I saw flames erupt from under my hood only a foot or two from my face, and said to Ellen, "We've got to get out, Sweetheart, the car's on fire." I do not remember releasing my seatbelt. But I know it was attached—and Ellen's too. If we were less modest we could show you the black and blue marks to prove it. Ellen's X-rays can show the broken sternum and several ribs to prove it.

Now I hate rules; especially laws that supposedly protect me from myself. I don't like the disciplines of self-restraint—including the discipline of seatbelt restraints. After all, we didn't have them when I was a kid. As a five-year-old I rode fearlessly standing on the seat with my arm around my dad's shoulder as he drove for days on end. But pressure from my wife, from my daughter, from my sister, not to mention from the State of Illinois, has made the practice of seatbelt self-restraint a matter of habit. Over time, this discipline of self-restraint has become, I suppose, a kind of virtue. I am now a person who quite "naturally" puts it on when I get into the car.

That night seven days ago reminded me that however paradoxical it may seem, the virtues of disciplined self-restraint and grace can be partners. I saw in that moment that self-discipline can be a means of grace; that Law can be a means of Grace. Our lives were spared. We don't know why, for we have long ago learned that while "to live is Christ, to die is gain." God apparently has more for Ellen and me to do in this world. But we take His sparing our lives, as evidence of His grace.

Christ did not come to this world to ignore the law, or to casually and indiscriminately dismiss the expectations of the Father. On the contrary, he took them with a deathly seriousness. If you are to be partakers of His grace, and become men and women of grace yourselves, I suggest that you begin by pursuing the virtue of discipline. Form good habits of study, of sexual conduct, of associations, and of spiritual formation. They will stand you in good stead as virtues for the season of examinations and the season of Christmas.

TEN

COURAGE: PAIN ANTICIPATING PAIN

JANUARY 27, 2003

It is good as always to see you all back safely from the holidays. I hope they were weeks of refreshment and renewal. I know many of you have made some exciting trips (Ireland, Dominican, Czech Republic, Tex-Mex) and I wish it were possible to hear your stories and see your pictures. These experiences are often life changing.

Over the past few weeks, I have been thinking a lot about fear. It seems that fear has entered the lives of many of those I love. Let me tell you about a few examples. First, my wife Ellen has developed a strong aversion—shall I call it fear—of traveling the Old National Trail road where we were nearly killed in our accident on December 1. I suppose it's a mild fear, but though I have driven it, she certainly has not traveled that road since.

Then, over Christmas, my wife and daughter and I visited our son in Croatia where he is living and working this year as a consultant for the U.S. government. The story of our trip over reads like a bad dream with cancelled flights, delayed flights, rerouted flights, lost luggage, and so on. Despite the fact my twenty-three-year-old daughter is an experienced world traveler, she burst into tears when en route to Budapest but coming from different points of origin we finally found one another over a paging system in Zurich where none of us had expected to be. The pressures of intense law school exams made the trauma of it all, and especially of catching her rearranged connection in JFK by only sixty seconds, very frightening.

While there, we noted that the people in Croatia and Hungary smiled very little. We joked about it, posing for deadpan pictures you can see on the web in what we called "eastern European style." But personal recollections of how bullet holes got in the walls of their own homes and many downtown buildings remind them the Serbo-Croatian war is very recent history, and the fear lingers.

My son felt fear at the end of our visit as we left him again, living alone to work in a difficult situation where he does not speak the language. He also felt a different kind of fear the day before we left after he proposed marriage to his girlfriend who was along with us for the holidays. It's frightening to take such a step! I remember the whole night after I proposed to Ellen, lying awake on the bed staring at the moon, saying over and over again, "My God what have I done?" "My God what have I done?" Like father like son, he too felt fear.

My daughter also felt fear from the impact of his proposal. She cried hard, feeling the fear that she was no longer the only daughter. Perhaps that seems an odd fear, but for any who have felt their special niche in any close group threatened you know it is a very real fear, coupled with loneliness and the fear of growing up.

My wife's fears have been compounded only in the last few days this week, as she visited her ailing father in Peoria. The doctor said he has "six months" and no matter how you think you've prepared yourself, it is still a shock, and it is still frightening; especially when your mom died when you were sixteen leaving this last parent.

My mother has felt fear too. Her failing memory gives her an odd objectless fear—fear of forgetting. Because what's forgotten is forgotten, her fear circles around on itself. It is the lonely fear of old age.

Some of you are seniors. Would you raise your hand if you're a senior? This may be the last semester of your college education. While it may seem impossible, it's coming to an end. It seemed to stretch out ahead of you forever when you started getting those information brochures in high schools—perhaps several each week even when you were a sophomore! But now it's coming, and the fears are legion. What am I going to do? Where am I going to work? Will I get a job? How can I live without my friends? Am I really that grown up?

I myself have certainly not been spared from fear either. Since fifteen years ago this month, there has been the fear of losing my wife. And since our accident before Christmas there has been fear this hip won't heal right and my life will be changed and limited. As I have watched the economy continue to stumble last fall, and now tumble even since a good start on the new year, my fears for the college mount. As a student in philosophy,

I never imagined that stock market charts could make my stomach hurt. With the crucial donations and enrollment applications for next year falling behind the pace we believe we need, I feel fear. And while it may seem an odd thing to confess, even as I read some challenging theology last week, I found myself frightened by the prospect it could be true, and if true, it called into question the faithfulness and reliability of God's promises. So, doubts are frightening too; in fact they can prompt some of the deepest fears.

I imagine my awareness of these fears all around me has been enhanced by some films I've seen. First were the ones from teaching COR 401. (Let me digress to say it was a wonderful course, full of all the challenges, ambiguities, pressures, conflicts, and disagreeable exchanges that make real life real.) We saw *Bowling for Columbine*, a powerful indictment claiming American culture is permeated by fear. It's not the guns, not the history, not the poverty, not the TV, not even Marilyn Manson that drives us to kill one another in numbers way out of proportion to our population. Instead, it is said to be our fear! The media feed it. "If it bleeds, it leads." And the movie industry helps too. With Ellen out of town, I found myself watching the *Blair Witch Project* on TV. It's all about fear. And in case I have not given you enough evidence that fear is all around us, try just joking in airport security! Or let me remind you the precarious worldwide nuclear "balance" is dangerously unstable in the Far East. Finally, I could hardly overlook the fact that right now a quarter of a million young American soldiers are wending their way eastward, leaving frightened families on piers and runways all around the country. The soldiers themselves of course are frightened too, with the prospects of war in Iraq foremost in their minds.

But what is fear? That probably sounds like a dumb question since everyone knows it when they feel it. But let me try a working definition. Fear is an emotion, an unpleasant emotion, that *usually* accompanies anticipation of something painful that *may* happen. The three key elements are that it is itself a bad feeling, that it occurs because we are thinking about the future, and the future we imagine is painful. In a nutshell, fear may be thought of as "the pain of anticipating pain."

The results of fear are varied. In the extreme it is literally deadly. An excess of fear can shut down our physical bodies more quickly than most of us can imagine unless we have felt such terror. In lesser forms it is distracting, upsetting, or even entirely paralyzing. Fear can paralyze your ability to speak in crucial moments or to write an exam for which you have studied. It can block other normal reactions too, causing you to respond with instinctual defensiveness rather than with gracious and open responses that might be more in character. It can show itself in a range of behaviors from anger and violence to withdrawal, silence, and depression. Some of these results of fear may have haunted you even already today!

As I have reflected these past weeks on the fear all around me, I have also reflected on how people respond. The virtue of character most often mentioned as the antidote to fear is *courage*. But then I have to ask, "What is courage?" The other night, again in Ellen's absence—she needs to be careful about leaving me alone too often don't you think?—I found myself squinting to watch *Rambo III* on a squirrelly cable channel we don't really get. I wanted to watch it because it seemed to be about as opposite to the *Blair Witch Project* as I could imagine. It was supposedly all about courage rather than fear. Well, as an aside I confess I was amazed by the irony of glorifying Afghans who now since 9/11 have been made villains for turning against us the same weapons we gave them back then. But watching the "Italian Stallion," it didn't take me long to figure out that Aristotle was right when he said, "He who exceeds in fearlessness...would be a sort of madman." You see Aristotle believed, "Courage is the *mean*, the middle place, with regard to the feelings of fear and confidence" (*Nicomachean Ethics Book II*). To be too full of fear is to be a coward. But to be too full of confidence is to be a fool. For John Rambo to face Russian tanks and troops with only two guns was not an act of courage.

Still the question remains, what then *is* real courage? Again let me try a working definition. Courage is not just another emotion; an antidote emotion to fear. Instead, courage is a quality of character that enables you to anticipate pain without the *usual* results, namely fear.

In the first place it is important to see this is an aspect of that notorious "character" you hear us talking about all the time here at Greenville

College. It's an aspect that makes it possible to respond in a different and more noble way under certain circumstances. Unless your character includes courage you'll respond in the usual way; fear. But shaping your character to include courage takes time, effort, and practice. It takes conscious decisions to choose the mean between fear and confidence. And it must be repeated habitually over and over to bend character to this shape. Without that repetition, our character will respond in the *usual* way to anticipated pain; i.e., with fear.

Second, courage comes into play really only when we already anticipate future pain. You can't really be courageous unless you are in a situation which makes pain seem likely. Of course, if you aren't smart enough to see what's likely coming, then you don't anticipate pain, so you can't be courageous. But for the most part, in our world today, thanks to both reality and the virtual reality of the media, we typically have such good imaginations we often anticipate pain, even when it really is *not* likely. This anticipation of pain, this fear, is pervasive, so the opportunities for courage are too!

But third, let's focus on what courage really produces. I have said it allows us to anticipate pain without the *usual* results. That usual result is fear. So, *some* would say it prevents the courageous person from even feeling the fear at all. Aristotle takes this view and says the courageous person "stands his ground against things that are terrible, and delights in this, or at least is not pained" (*Nicomachean Ethics Book II*). But if this be courage, I suspect there are not many brave souls among us because I think not feeling fear is really rare. *Others* suggest that courage means feeling the fear, but not showing it. Somehow it seems to me that this is not courage, but merely bravado, a close cousin but not really the same noble virtue at all. So, finally, it seems to me, that perhaps since the usual result of anticipating pain is a fear that paralyzes us, it might be that real courage results not in *avoiding* fear, or *masking* fear, but in allowing us to *feel it without paralysis*. In short, courage, lets us anticipate pain yet *keep on going*.

When we get up in the morning frightened by the prospects of the day, something I think we all feel or have felt, it takes courage to get up anyway. When we walk into the room for that exam for which we've labored to prepare, frightened by the prospects of failure, it takes courage to walk in anyway. When we confess our love to another, frightened by the prospects of rejection, it takes courage to confess it anyway. When we confront a friend with constructive criticism, frightened by the prospect of loneliness, it takes courage to confront anyway. When we have to decide which job to take and where to move, frightened by the prospect of the unknown and unfamiliar, it takes courage to decide anyway. When we walk out of the doctor's office, frightened by the prospect of death, it takes courage to walk out and on anyway. While some may disagree, I believe it's not that we do not feel the fear, but rather that we go on in spite of it. That is courage. Theologian Paul Tillich described it as the courage to be "in spite of" our fear of specific things and even "in spite of" our anxiety that has no specific object.

Now I suppose I could stop right here. *Courage is going on in spite of fear.* But as I thought about talking to you about courage, as a follower of Jesus Christ, I had to ask, "What does Scripture say about courage?" I admit I found the answer pretty surprising. Of course, the Old Testament is full of references to courage. It most often refers to the courage required in war; as in the experience of God's people when they considered entering the Promised Land at Zin. They were exhorted to "fear not" but to be of good courage (Numbers 13:20, Deuteronomy 1:21, 31:6 NIV). It seems they too were often a nation of fear as we may be today. In those instances where it does not refer to battle, it often exhorts leaders to hold firm to the law of God and to their resolve to reform God's people. Joshua is told as a leader, "Be strong and of good courage" (Joshua 1:9 KJV) so that the people of God will prosper. And David challenging his son Solomon again urges him to "Be strong and of good courage" (1 Chronicles 28:20 RSV) adding that Solomon should "fear not, be not dismayed, for the Lord God, even my God is with you. He will not fail you or forsake you..." (1 Chron. 28:20 RSV). And the prophet Azariah challenged King Asa to take courage as he undertook the destruction of idols throughout the land (2 Chron. 15:8). Again, when Ezra the priest was commanded to reform God's people he was told to take courage and do it (Ezra 10:4). And finally, David ends several of his Psalms with the call to "Wait on the LORD: be of good courage, and he will strengthen thine heart..." (Psalms 27:14, 31:24 KJV).

But when I combed the New Testament, at least in the King James Version, I found no use of the word *courage* in the Gospels at all, and in fact it is used only once in the entire New Testament. In Acts 28:15, when Paul was traveling under guard to Rome he neared the city and was greeted by Christians at the Three Taverns on Via Appia where he took courage! This absence of reference made me begin to wonder if courage is merely a humanistic construction, exalted especially among Greeks who wrote about it constantly. Perhaps it is a counterfeit response to the anticipation of fear, an inappropriate response for followers of Christ.

So, I began to look for references to fear instead, to see how God's Word calls followers of Christ to respond. Almost immediately I was drawn to 1 John, because as a young boy I remember going to the altar and recommitting my life to Christ time after time fearful that somehow I was not yet really "saved." 1 John is a book of reassurance, speaking directly to the problem of fear out of abundant references to God's love. John confirms as we already know that fear has to do with pain ("punishment" 4:18 RSV) but then adding that "he who fears is not perfected in love" (4:18 RSV) and repeats himself on this crucial matter saying, "There is no fear in love, but perfect love casts out all fear" (4:18 RSV). It struck me that it's not so much that the proposed human Greek solution to fear in courage is wrong, but that God provides a deeper answer that tells us how to find that courage; it is found in love.

How does this work? I began to wonder what does love have to do with courage? I began to review those examples of fear I shared with you at the beginning. What is it that gives courageous people courage? What gives them the strength to face those fears without paralysis? Perhaps it really is love. For the soldier it is the love of country, and maybe even love of family. The same love may inspire the politician who chooses to take a courageous but unpopular stand. For my son, facing the fears of marriage, it is the love of his fiancée Lyla. With my daughter in tears on my shoulder fearing her anticipated "loss" of that special place in her brother's eyes, and her special place in the family, it was the reminder of her love for her brother that gave her courage. For me as I often struggle to face the fears of my work, it is the love of my family, the love for what Greenville College has done in the life of my father, my sister, my brother-in-law, and the love

I have for the transforming process we pursue here that keeps me going. But perhaps the most powerful example of courage in my life is that of my wife Ellen. She faces fear every day but gets up and keeps going. It seems to be her love for me, for her children, and even for life itself that gives her courage. So, it seems love *is* tied to courage, in a way I might not have imagined. Love inspires courage to face fear and go on.

But perfect love seems daunting. If it is "perfect love" that "casts out all fears" I want it. But how can I ever find perfect love? Surely, it's not by my own efforts! So, I am left once again with fear in parts of my life. But John yet again brings us the "good word" of our loving God when he says, "*If we love one another, God abides in us and his love is perfected in us*" (1 John 4:12 RSV). In other words, it is not *our* love, but *His* love that is perfected in us. Our task is merely to love one another the best way we can and then he will abide in us, His Spirit perfecting His love within us so all fears will be cast away. I thank God this morning that we can love because he first loved us (4:19 RSV) and because of this we can be people of courageous character.

What is the most courageous thing you have ever done? Where are you being called to be courageous today? As you face the fears of your day, of your semester, of your life, focus on loving those around you. I mean really loving them. In this way *then* His abiding love will provide you the courage perhaps not to avoid the fear but to go on nevertheless; to go on "in spite of the fear." Love one another, then be strong and of good courage this day.

ELEVEN

DISCIPLINE: WHAT PETE TOLD ME TO TALK ABOUT

MAY 5, 2003

Introduction...

Last Tuesday night I hobbled over to Holtwick lounge around 9:30 just to talk with anyone who wanted to talk. I always enjoy these evenings. Last week the group was small, so I asked how everyone's studies were going. My friend Pete—are you here today, Pete?—told me things weren't too bad but he had a speech on Monday. I asked about his and then said I also had a speech on Monday—this one I'm giving right now! I said I didn't really know at that time what I'd talk about except I wanted to talk about a "virtue"—meaning some specific quality of character—instead of just "character in general." When I talked to you in January I had talked about the virtue of "courage." So, I asked Pete what he suggested. He said three things. First, he said, talk about "discipline" since at this time of the year with examinations looming, that's the virtue most of us wish we had more of! Second, he said tell us something personal. Third—no I'll wait till the end to tell you the third thing he said. So, my topic today is, "Discipline" or "What Pete Told Me to Talk About."

Prayer...

Will you bow your heads with me for prayer please?

> May the words of my mouth, and the meditations of our hearts, be acceptable in thy sight, oh Lord, our Strength and our Redeemer.

Examinations...

It's exam time! My daughter called an hour ago asking Ellen and me to pray for her. She's a second year law student and taking the first of her finals as I speak. Many years ago, it was the fall of 1969 and I was a junior in college. Exam time for me had never been easy. In high school in Brazil, our exams had always been cumulative three hour affairs, two each day for three days in a row. Even then, I was always a nervous wreck preparing and thought they'd never end. It was back then in high school that I first learned to say to myself, "Remember, Jim, no matter how painful and interminable they may seem, these next three days will take no longer to pass by than any other three days!" Somehow that helped. But now in 1969, in college it seemed the pressure was just too much. I had already been awake without sleep for more than forty-eight hours, literally studying the entire time. I felt like a failure since the more I studied the more convinced I was that I didn't know anything at all! I was sure I would fail the exams. Honestly, I'd felt that way before virtually every other exam in college before. But this time I just knew it was going to be true! The war in Vietnam was at a climax. The previous spring semester, all our classes had to be made "Pass/Fail" because massive student demonstrations had shut down the major universities, blocked major highways, and for several days, paralyzed the streets outside my dorm and the very city of Boston itself. This added pressure because most of us were in school on "student deferments." Failing exams meant a mandatory trip to Southeast Asia almost immediately. And it most certainly didn't help our feeling of pressure that just the month before, our sister dormitory across the street had lived up to its reputation once again. East Campus, as that dorm was called, had only single rooms, and housed the brightest and also the loneliest, most eccentric of my fellow students at M.I.T. It also had the highest suicide rate of any dorm on a campus with the highest suicide rate in the nation. This time they had only thought to break into his room because of the smell. That memory was fresh, so the pressure was almost unbearable.

When I dragged myself to the exam hall, I couldn't help but recall that only a few weeks before it had been "taken over" by the Weathermen, a militant student branch of the SDS (Students for a Democratic Society) and used for civil disobedience training. It was a huge National Guard Armory, with seventy-five-foot ceilings and glaring arena lights. Our individual exam tables were each about three feet square, and spaced precisely around the floor, in endless rows, for hundreds of students in our physics course.

As we nervously awaited instructions and the question sheets, one student came in almost too late, running down the row of tables, echoing across the hardwood floors in the nearly quiet hall. In his hand was a six-pack of beer. Within minutes the hall was deathly quiet except the rustle of papers. We soon realized that the questions were so difficult it seemed they could only have been written by a demon. Ten minutes into the exam, the latecomer, popped a beer can open, and we heard him guzzle. Ten minutes later, he opened and consumed another. One after another, we were all counting—like bullets in a revolver. Half an hour or so after the last can had been consumed, our "friend" screamed at the top of his lungs, "I just can't take it anymore!!!," rose, and ran noisily out of the hall. How we ever finished that exam I will never know! But I think it had something to do with discipline. And that's what I'd like to talk to you about today. By the way, you may be happy to know, it turned out later our "friend" was actually not in our class at all, but a senior, who somehow got past the proctors and the system, and into the exam for the sole purpose of unnerving the rest of us. He absolutely succeeded!

Definitions of Discipline...

It is one of our goals at Greenville College to transform students for lives of character. Excellence of character requires the deliberate intentional cultivation of virtues, including that of discipline.

So, what is discipline? The Oxford English Dictionary distinguishes the noun and the verb. In other words, discipline can be both something you *have* and something you *do*; an example of the distinction we make here at Greenville between *being* and *doing* when we talk about character and service. Like most cases of being and doing they are really inseparable.

To *have* discipline is to *have knowledge or skill or instruction that conforms to an order or controlled system.* Drs. Huston, Ross, and Dunkley, for example, have disciplines. Their knowledge, as well as their methods of thinking and research embody the disciplines of history, communication, and microbiology. You are each beginning to have a discipline; it's your major. Your knowledge of facts and methods in one area are conforming to an order: for example, of music, psychology, or philosophy. The same could be said for our track and cross-country team or Tom Landry's old Cowboy football team. I'm told the genius of his "flex" defense was that they had a disciplined orderly set of controlled behaviors.

On the other hand, to *perform* discipline is to instruct, educate, train; more especially, to train to habits of order and subordination; to bring under control. So, the GC faculty and coaches, like old coach Landry, also perform discipline when they work to bring their students or their players under their disciplines. Parents do this all the time too, disciplining their children. And of course, you can also perform discipline on yourself—self-discipline—when you train yourself and bring yourself under control in some area of thought or behavior.

When I searched Amazon.com for *discipline* as a keyword, it showed 32,000 books! Barnes and Noble shows 2,686 books with the word *discipline* in the actual title! One such book my wife and I used in raising our children was by Dr. James Dobson, entitled, *Dare to Discipline*. I haven't seen it recently so maybe our kids threw it out!

Two other books have shaped my thinking about spiritual disciplines, an area we may sometimes not connect with the idea of discipline at all. One is *Spirit of the Disciplines*, by Dallas Willard, and another is *Celebration of Disciplines*, by Willard's disciple, Richard Foster. Obviously even the word "disciple," from the same roots as "discipline," suggests how one person works to conform their life to the pattern and order of another's life. In *Spirit of the Disciplines*, Willard tells us that disciplines are behaviors we practice, to put ourselves after a time, in a place where God can do in or through us what we could not have done on our own otherwise. In other words, from a spiritual perspective, discipline is not an end in itself—something to our eternal credit, something that earns our salvation—but merely a means, a tool, that allows God to work in us and through us more effectively. I pray that many of you practice the spiritual disciplines of private prayer, reading the Bible, silence, and others.

So, when we say a person of character has the virtue of *discipline*, what do they look like? They are people who have learned that if they want to excel, they must concentrate their freedom in one area by being willing to constrain their freedoms in other areas.

> Lanny Bassham, Olympic gold medalist in small bore rifle competition, tells what concentration does for his marksmanship: "Our sport is controlled nonmovement. We are shooting from 50 meters—over half a football field—at a bull's eye three-quarters the size of a dime. If the angle of error at the point of the barrel is more than five one thousandths of an inch, you drop into the next circle and lose a point. So, we have to learn how to make everything stop. I stop my breathing. I stop my digestion by not eating for 12 hours before the competition. I train by running to keep my pulse around 60, so I have a full second between beats—I have gotten it lower but found that the stroke-volume increased so much that each beat really jolted me. You do all of this and you have the technical control. But you also have to have some years of experience in reading conditions: the wind, the mirage. Then you have the other 80 percent of the problems— the mind. Without strenuous discipline, winning the Olympic gold in small bore rifle competition would be impossible. (*Sports Illustrated* 8/2/76, pp. 31–35)

It is tempting these days to suppose that true freedom comes from maximizing our ability to "do what we please." That could not be further from the truth. The reality is that real freedom comes from concentration and constraint. My father was a preacher and used to talk about the goldfish who objected to the constraints of the fishbowl, bemoaning its limits and yearning for freedom. How much better life would be without these walls! As he grew, he struggled to escape and finally, in a lucky leap jumped out only to discover of course that the constraints of the bowl were the very secret of his freedom.

Ellen and I used to read a similar story to our children; the story of "Tootle the Train." Like the goldfish, Tootle, dreamed of wandering "freely" in the meadows full of flowers and butterflies. But when he escaped the constraints of the tracks, he found his ability to move severely limited. Those apparently limiting constraints had in fact been the secret of his ability to concentrate or maximize his efforts, and move as he was designed to move, quickly and effectively.

These are simple almost laughable stories, but the principle is sound. Discipline means constraining or limiting our efforts in one area so we can concentrate them more effectively. This means, paradoxically, constraint actually brings freedom. You knew there had to be paradox in my comments today right?!

You athletes among us are perhaps the ones most able to understand this. You concentrate your attention, limiting or constraining your freedom to eat, to party, to sleep in, to socialize and so on, in order to submit to the order or training that actually frees you up to perform more effectively on the field. That's why you can be examples to the rest of us about discipline. But this lesson, this paradox of discipline, applies to just about everything: to studies, to relationships, to eating, to sexuality, and of course to our life with Christ.

But discipline is not the only virtue we need to be people of good character. If we constrain ourselves or allow others to constrain us to the wrong path, we may become disciplined in bad ways. We become masters of pain and cruelty, monsters in marriage or business for example. Naturally, the choice of which constraints we follow is crucial. Choose carefully the constraints you adopt. As a disciple, choose carefully the person you follow.

Patience and Persistence...

A person of discipline is then someone who has learned to constrain their freedom so they can concentrate their ability. But there are at least two other virtues that go along with discipline, so closely they are like its shadows.

The first is *patience*. A disciplined person is also almost always patient. Another way of putting this is to say the disciplined person has learned to delay gratification. They are willing to sacrifice now in order to gain later.

They recognize that in the "bank of life" one must make deposits before you can make withdrawals. It is perhaps one of the greatest fears I have for us all, that in a day when credit card offers come in the mail almost daily, when we prefer "microwavable" food and scratch off instant jackpot lotteries, and when our attitude is "buy now, pay later," we have lost the ability to be patient, to delay gratification and with it, our ability to be disciplined. The result of course is that we do not constrain ourselves, and consequently do not reap the benefits of concentration and excellence in our lives. I'm reminded of the Fram oil filter commercials urging people to invest a little more now in their higher quality oil filters in order to save a lot more later on repairs. The mechanic says, "Pay me now, or pay me later." How are you with delayed gratification? Do you study first and play later? Can you wait until the weekend to spend time with friends?

A second virtue tied closely to discipline is *persistence*. Discipline cannot be learned quickly. As Richard Carpenter put it in his song, it requires "years and years of practice." And as many long-distance runners realize, it is often lonely. In January I spoke to you about courage and said it means "going on in spite of fear." In one sense, discipline is just plain "going on;" no matter what.

In the summer of 1979, I participated in *Innoculum*, the Westmont College version of *Walkabout*. With eight freshmen students, I hiked for ten days in the mountainous backcountry of Yosemite National Park. It was complete with technical rope work, glacial terrain, and a frightening solo experience. Near the end of the trip, we tackled a one-hundred foot vertical cliff with the plan to rappel back down. One by one we would free climb the cliff, then thrill at bouncing our way back down on rope belay. That was the plan. I will never forget the sensation of climbing hard for thirty minutes only to find myself in a position where it seemed I could neither go up or down. I was exhausted, panicky, and of course too well aware of my students below holding my rope and shouting encouragement to me. It crossed my mind that I had no business clinging to the face of a rock cliff holding on with my fingernails to nubbins of rock no larger than tiny pebbles. I would never have made it without that encouragement from below. But because of it, I somehow found the strength to persist; to just keep going on. It's hard to describe the "high" I felt in reaching the top. The sheer exhilaration and self-confidence were amazing. Discipline requires persistence.

In the last semester of my senior year of college, I worked in my laboratory or my single dorm room, to finish a senior thesis. My schedule included only one class and because the optics lab vibrated from Boston subways during the day, my lab work could only be done at night. In other words, I rarely saw anyone else! I remember one night panicking after weeks of trying to write. My mind felt like mush. My thoughts were confused and jumbled from too much effort. Like that moment on the cliff many years later, it seemed I could go on no further. I remember leaving my desk, stepping back to my bed in the tiny room. Kneeling by the bed I literally squeezed my head hard between my hands, trying to physically force the ideas from my brain as I struggled to organize and think my way through the problem I was writing about. It was a breakthrough moment in that semester and even in my life. I stretched myself and saw I was capable of much more than I had imagined.

Fortunately, such moments requiring sheer mental or physical persistence don't occur that often, because they are incredibly draining. But to this day when I find myself exhausted and at my wits end, it still helps me to remember that excellence at almost anything, usually only comes at the cost of discipline that is doggedly persistent. Sometimes that means just showing up and continuing to show up. Woody Allen is reported to have said that showing up is eighty percent of success. I've heard others say showing up is fifty percent of the battle, ninety percent of helping, eighty percent of customer satisfaction, and according to Avis Miller, a Jewish writer, showing up is ninety percent of life!

Scripture...

There are of course many places where the Bible speaks of discipline. In 1 Corinthians 9:24, we read about the discipline of the athlete who avoids "sloppy living." The *Message* paraphrase puts it this way,

You've all been to the stadium and seen the athletes race. Everyone runs; one wins. Run to win. [25]All good athletes train hard. They do it for a gold medal that tarnishes and fades. You're after one that's gold eternally. [26]I don't know about you, but I'm running hard for the finish line. I'm giving it everything I've got. No sloppy living for me! [27]I'm staying alert and in top condition. I'm not going to get caught napping, telling everyone else all about it and then missing out myself.

In equally blunt language, Proverbs 12 says, "*Whoever loves discipline loves knowledge, but he who hates correction is stupid*" (Proverbs 12:1, RSV). Hebrews 12 connects discipline to the athlete but also to our relationship with our heavenly Father:

My dear child, don't shrug off God's discipline, but don't be crushed by it either. [6]It's the child he loves that he disciplines; the child he embraces, he also corrects. [7]God is educating you; that's why you must never drop out. He's treating you as dear children. This trouble you're in isn't punishment; it's training, [8]the normal experience of children. Only irresponsible parents leave children to fend for themselves. Would you prefer an irresponsible God? [9]We respect our own parents for training and not spoiling us, so why not embrace God's training so we can truly live? [10]While we were children, our parents did what seemed best to them. But God is doing what is best for us, training us to live God's holy best. [11]At the time, discipline isn't much fun. It always feels like it's going against the grain. Later, of course, it pays off handsomely, for it's the well-trained who find themselves mature in their relationship with God. [12]So don't sit around on your hands! No more dragging your feet! [13]Clear the path for long-distance runners so no one will trip and fall, so no one will step in a hole and sprain an ankle. Help each other out. And run for it" (Hebrews 12:5–12, MSG)!

In 2 Timothy 1 Paul reminds his student Timothy:

> For this reason, I am reminding you to fan into flame the gift of God, which is in you through the laying on of my hands. For God did not give us a spirit of timidity, but a spirit of power, love and self-discipline. (vv. 6–7, ISV).

Discipline of the Tongue...

Perhaps the most interesting reference to discipline in Scripture came to my attention in an odd way. The Oxford English Dictionary provides quotations for each word in the English language. They trace the word to its earliest known printed use. I was surprised to learn that the earliest printed use of the word *disciplined* is from 1384, when John Wycliffe, father of the English Reformation, and some say of English literature in general, translated the Bible into English for the first time. Wycliffe Bible Translators carry his name even today! Until then the Bible was available only in Latin and only to priests. The Oxford Dictionary cites as the earliest printed use of this word in this sense, it's use by Wycliffe in the epistle of James 3:13: *"Who is wise and disciplined among you?"* (OED, "disciplined, adj.") In the NIV, this verse goes on to say, *"Let them show it by...deeds done in the humility that comes from wisdom."*

What I find interesting about this passage, is how the author uses it to illustrate discipline. He makes the point that discipline is required if faith is to show itself in our deeds. Remember, James tells us faith without deeds is not even real faith. In particular, James believes that one part of our life is the hardest of all to discipline. It is the tongue. Using ancient analogies, he likens it to the rudder of a ship that is tiny yet turns the entire vessel in the face of the fiercest winds. He likens it also to the bit in the mouth of a horse. With only small movements it moves that large animal in one direction or another. Finally, he likens the tongue to a spark of fire. In some of the strongest language possible James warns us that the tongue, when left undisciplined, can through the smallest word, *"set a forest ablaze, ruin the world, turn harmony to chaos, throw mud on a reputation, send the whole world up in smoke and go up in smoke with it, smoke right from the pit of hell"* (James 3:6 Message).

In closing, I would like to read this entire passage from the book of James. It suggests that discipline, especially of the tongue, is central to Christian virtue. I read it to you as students of Greenville College. I read it especially to my colleagues the faculty at Greenville College during recent difficult days of disagreements on campus. I read it to us all as disciples of Christ, seeking by His Spirit to discipline our lives into conformity with the image of Jesus Christ. Ye who have ears, let him hear!

Don't be in any rush to become a teacher, my friends. Teaching is highly responsible work. Teachers are held to the strictest standards. [2]And none of us is perfectly qualified. We get it wrong nearly every time we open our mouths. If you could find someone whose speech was perfectly true, you'd have a perfect person, in perfect control of life. [3]A bit in the mouth of a horse controls the whole horse. [4]A small rudder on a huge ship in the hands of a skilled captain sets a course in the face of the strongest winds. [5]A word out of your mouth may seem of no account, but it can accomplish nearly anything—or destroy it! It only takes a spark, remember, to set off a forest fire. [6]A careless or wrongly placed word out of your mouth can do that. By our speech we can ruin the world, turn harmony to chaos, throw mud on a reputation, send the whole world up in smoke and go up in smoke with it, smoke right from the pit of hell. [7]This is scary: You can tame a tiger, [8]but you can't tame a tongue—it's never been done. The tongue runs wild, a wanton killer. [9]With our tongues we bless God our Father; with the same tongues we curse the very men and women he made in his image. [10]Curses and blessings out of the same mouth! My friends, this can't go on. [11]A spring doesn't gush fresh water one day and brackish the next, does it? [12]Apple trees don't bear strawberries, do they? Raspberry bushes don't bear apples, do they? You're not going to dip into a polluted mud hole and get a cup of clear, cool water, are you? [13]Do you want to be counted wise, to build a reputation for [discipline?] wisdom? Here's what you do: Live well, live wisely, live humbly. It's the way you live, not the way you talk, that counts. [14]Mean-spirited ambition isn't wisdom. Boasting that you are wise isn't wisdom. Twisting the truth to make yourselves sound wise isn't wisdom. [15]It's the furthest thing from wisdom—it's animal cunning, devilish conniving. [16]Whenever you're trying to look better than others or get the better of others, things fall apart and everyone ends up at the others' throats. [17]Real wisdom, God's wisdom, begins with a holy life and is characterized by getting along with others. It is gentle and reasonable, overflowing with mercy and blessings, not hot one day and cold the next, not two-faced. [18]You can develop a healthy, robust community that lives right with God and enjoy its results only if you do the hard work of getting along with each other, treating each other with dignity and honor (James 3:1-18 *The Message*).

Again, I say, "Ye who have ears, let him hear!

When I began this morning, I told you Pete suggested I do three things. First, talk to you about discipline. Second, include a personal story or two. And I promised to tell you the third thing. He said, "They will love you if you let them out half an hour early." Pete, I've tried my best. But I confess I've failed on the last one. Maybe two out of three isn't too bad?!

Let us pray!

TWELVE

TRUTH: THE FIRST CASUALTY

DECEMBER 1, 2003

For the last two weeks I've been thinking about what I'd like to share with you today. I thought about it especially as I met last week with some of your friends in Mozambique in class discussion, over lunch and coffee at an outdoor café, and even walking the warm Indian Ocean beach. By the way, they send their greetings, and expect to be back home this week! I thought about what I'd like to share with you as Ellen and I shared breakfast with good friends in our favorite café in Harare, Zimbabwe just Saturday morning. And I had a *lot* of time to think about it during forty hours of nonstop travel this weekend, including in the middle of the night, squeezed between Ellen and a South African nuclear engineer on the seventeen-hour flight from Johannesburg yesterday. I remember landing at the Cape Verde island in the mid-Atlantic Saturday night, but don't remember taking off from it again. And my body has no idea what time it is right now!

A number of thoughts have been pushing and pulling about in my mind. First, as you know, I like to talk about paradox; because I believe intellectual, moral, and spiritual life is generally more complex than it seems. I want Greenville graduates to know how to embrace both passionate commitment and reflective self-criticism. That's what the liberating arts are about. But second, for the past year, I've also felt it's not enough just to talk about paradox in general. Instead, I believe from time to time we must think carefully about the specific and often paradoxical virtues of character we are all working to develop. Consequently, over the past months I have spoken to you about Discipline, about Courage, and even about Grace. In fact, in speaking to you a year ago this week my topic of Grace arose from a life changing experience. Ellen and I had narrowly escaped death in an automobile accident a year ago tonight. Grace was also appropriate last year because of a third factor that has pushed and pulled about in my mind this week again. It was the Christmas season, even as it is now, and Christmas is surely about Grace—God's gift of grace in the amazing birth, life, death, and resurrection of our Lord Jesus. This week I've asked myself, "What paradoxical virtue might be appropriate for our reflection together this Christmas season? Love is an obvious candidate. It is certainly a virtue, certainly at the heart of Christmas, and is certainly often paradoxical.

Christmas is about the arrival of God's grace and love; for Christ is grace and love in the flesh. But my experiences of the past few weeks suggest another Christmas virtue instead. Christmas is also about the arrival of Truth, for Christ is the Way, the Truth, and the Life. So, I'd like to share with you a few thoughts about truth.

My conversations with South African, Mozambican, and Zimbabwean friends these past days have reminded me of that familiar saying that, "In war, the first casualty is always truth." The twenty-year physical civil war in Mozambique is over and it's deeply satisfying for me to see the country for which I have prayed daily for ten years regaining stability and developing rapidly. Likewise, the long South African struggle for majority rule has been won, and despite high crime rates and the huge task to reduce the gaps between rich and poor, the trends seem positive. But in Zimbabwe, where fifteen years ago, Ellen and I took our children to live for two years, the picture is not so good. It is a jewel of a country, full of warmhearted people, amazing animals, and mind clearing landscapes to which we have become deeply attached. Yet for the past few years, beneath an external surface of "normalcy" there is a kind of war underway, growing more threatening each month. And it seems that truth has been the first among the victims that in one way or another sadly also include just about everyone; from long-term white residents to the poorest blacks.

In my conversations I found myself asking the same two or three questions over and over to everyone I met. "How do people survive with 600–800 percent inflation!?", "How many Zimbabweans live outside the country; in self-imposed exile?", "What is the HIV infection rate?", "Is there food in the country to eat?", "Are people being denied their legal and human rights to property and even safety?", "How long before the eighty-year-old president of twenty years will step down?" I asked my white friends, my black friends, my Christian friends, and even some who were neither Christians nor especially my friends. While the picture that emerged is bleak regardless of what numbers you believe, the most discouraging thing to see was that no one seemed to be able to agree; even about what seemed to be fairly factual matters. [Update 2020: *It is hard not to see a comparable loss of truth in America. CNN/Fox, NYT/WaPo, skepticism, cynicism, and with this loss, the devolution of politics into little more than a "will to power."*]

On inflation, the rate is at least 560 percent if you believe the outside press, or 800 percent if you believe my friend who is shadow minister of economics in the opposition party. While it's the worst in the world, government officials point out it's only gotten bad since July and say things will change.

How do people survive when costs can double in a week? It can take a backpack to carry the bills needed to buy simple personal things. My friends do business with pickup trucks full of money. And salaries cannot possibly keep pace. Lifelong retirement plans are worthless paying the equivalent of USD$10 per month, about the cost of a single shirt or blouse. One theory is that they survive on money earned by family and friends who work outside Zimbabwe and pass these earnings back in inflation proof foreign currency like U.S. dollars, British pounds, or South African rand. This in turn raises the question of how many do this. I heard as few as twenty percent and as many as thirty-five percent of all Zimbabweans are in this "diaspora." Another theory on how they survive says it's not foreign currency that keeps people going, but they are just "cutting back." People cannot afford bus fares to come to work so they walk for hours each day. Two former colleagues of mine, both with Ph.Ds. and a lifetime of experience, cannot afford eggs or cheese and eat potatoes only once a month.

What about HIV? I have heard as few as twenty percent and as many as forty percent of the population is infected. With life expectancy down dramatically to only forty-two years and population growth the lowest in Africa and dropping fast, the number of AIDS orphans is said to be skyrocketing; yet I didn't see the crowds of street kids I was told I'd see.

On whether there is food, some despair that once a net exporter of food to Africa only ten years ago, Zimbabwe now cannot feed itself and 800–1000 people are dying every day of starvation. Yet the streets of Harare are busy, filled with BMWs and Mercedes and SUVs, people are well-dressed, the stores are full, and unlike previous experience, Ellen and I had no beggars approach us—except two homeless white men—an amazing turnabout from older colonial days.

On the question of legal and human rights, some of my own friends share stories of illegal occupations of farms, groundless harassment or imprisonment, and physical beatings—even by police. Yet other friends serve in high places, wrestle with the moral dilemmas of helping their people while avoiding the taint of corruption themselves and discount the horror stories. They point out that the picture is not that simple and help me engage city officials who offer gracious hospitality and assistance to me as I explore the development of Greenville study programs in Zimbabwe.

When will the president step down? He is under fire from the U.S. for "stealing the election" in 2001 and Zimbabwe has been suspended by his own Commonwealth partners for disregard of the laws and unacceptable restraints on free press. Some say he could step down as early as this December when his ZANU party meets, or even on his birthday in February. Other friends who are politically active and very knowledgeable about Zimbabwe differed widely. Some told me eighteen months without doubt, and others are preparing to join the exodus of multigenerational whites from that country in the belief it will be another ten years before change comes. [Update 2020: *Mugabe remained as president another fourteen years! A coup in 2017 replaced him with the current president Mnangagwa who has literally changed nothing. Mugabe's death two years later in 2019 left a nation as bad off as before. Friends in Zimbabwe in 2020 say it is worse than ever!*]

It was amazing to me to see the variety of perspectives on what was happening; without any obvious way for me or for anyone to determine the truth! The government has mandated what most Westerners view as unconscionable restraints on the press and public gatherings. Yet others reply they were laws enacted through the legal process of the country. Still others respond that the processes themselves are deeply corrupted and even the government disregards its own legal branch. As I told my friends as I neared the end of my visit, the only thing for certain was the deep and troubling uncertainty. Truth is the casualty of this economic, political, and cultural war.

If you permit a digression, when I tried to find the source of the statement that truth is the first casualty of war, I found not one, but *eight* different "answers." These included the Greek poet Aeschylus, Rudyard Kipling, Winston Churchill, Arthur Ponsby, several unknown individuals, and most likely, either U.S. Senator Hiram Johnson in a 1918 speech or Samuel Johnson in a 1758 magazine article. How ironic that even the truth about who first said "truth is the first casualty" is itself a casualty!

So last week it was very appropriate that I should find myself meeting at 6 a.m. in Beira, Mozambique with Mandy, one of our Greenville in Africa students, to talk about "postmodernism." Appropriate because postmodernism is all about this dilemma of truth. It's all about the tension—or call it the paradox—between believing there *is* truth to be known and actually knowing *what* that truth may be. Like the old story about several people holding different parts of an elephant and proclaiming only their perspective was the truth, the temptation is to hear the endless perspectives of my friends and throw up my hands and say there is no truth about Zimbabwe today.

Some would say that is precisely what the leadership of Zimbabwe wants to achieve. Because when truth is a casualty, only force remains. Fredrich Nietzsche described this situation by saying that when truth is lost, all that remains is the will to power. For those who wish to control others, especially for their own personal gain, the first step of war is deliberately to make truth the first casualty. Laws which prohibit open inquiry, prohibit open communication, prohibit dissent, leave everyone blind, destroy truth, and end in a battle for power. Some have said the deepest issue in Zimbabwe is not the economic turmoil…that could easily end with renewed investment. Nor is it political affiliations as there are good and bad in every group. But it is the loss of the rule of law; when the ability to know the truth of what is really going on means law is replaced by power alone. Truth is the casualty.

But what is the paradox? And where is the Christmas story here?

The paradox comes in learning to know the truth without controlling it. As followers of Jesus Christ, and unlike many postmodernists, we do not abandon the idea that there is Truth—that in fact he IS the Truth—merely because we understand that in this life our understandings of this truth will vary. But as His followers we *are* postmodern because we recognize that there are perspectives and differing points of view; not only about Zimbabwean politics but about important issues even related to our faith. We accept this because the Bible tells us that "Now we see through a glass darkly," and only then "face to face." What this means is that we must be very careful not to substitute power or force for Truth. We risk doing this when we try to control the truth by insisting that our version of it is the only acceptable version. We are tempted to "package" the marvelous Truth of Christ; to control it, capture it, confine it, for fear we will lose it. But paradoxically, when we try to control the truth, confine it, restrict it; we lose it. In this life we cannot "own" the Truth. As with the political and economic wars of Zimbabwe, or Nietzsche's "will to power," when in our petty daily human and often even religious wars for control, we allow power to dominate, Truth is the first casualty.

The secret for handling this paradox is found in the Christmas story. That Christmas story is of course that Jesus Christ is the Truth. All of us have sinned and fall short of what God designed us to be. But God sent His only Son to this world as an infant child, to live among us, full of grace and truth. By the sacrifice of His life, and His resurrection we can be put back into right relation with our Creator, with others, with the world, and even with our own selves. When this Truth comes into our lives, we are set free from the oppression that always arises when truth has been made a casualty of the "war" around us and within us.

Because the Christmas story tells us that Truth is not *about* a person but *is* a Person, our relationship to the truth should be different. It is easier to understand how to know truth without controlling it and killing it if Truth is a person. For most of us we can understand why we should not package, control, or even own another person, while nevertheless still knowing them well, even intimately. This faith in a person we call trust. So, in this Christmas season, let us seek the virtue of Truth in our lives. In the cultural and community and personal wars we fight, let us know Him who is Truth. Let us trust Him. Let us work to avoid replacing Truth with power.

THIRTEEN

HOPE II: SOUTH AFRICAN AIRWAYS

DECEMBER 1, 2004

It is good to see you this morning. I want to talk to you for a few minutes about Hope. There are several reasons for my choice of topic. First, for the past two years I've tried to use these opportunities in chapel to say a few things about some of the virtues that make up a person of good character. We talk often at Greenville College about education for character, and much of that kind of education occurs in the subtle almost unconscious dynamics of personal relationships among faculty, staff, and students in our community. But other than pointing as often as possible to the character of Jesus Christ, it's not often that we stop and reflect intentionally about what kind of character we are really seeking for ourselves. I have had occasion to speak about the virtues of truth, of courage, of faith, and even of discipline. Today I'd like to say something about hope.

Second, in fact, hope may well be the single most important virtue that should characterize Christians in general! Paul reminds us in Ephesians that "There is one Body and one Spirit, just as you were called to the one hope..." (Ephesians 4:4 RSV)! So, unless we're constantly thinking about hope we may be missing out on the very thing which should distinguish us as followers of Jesus Christ!

But this leads to a third reason for my choice. That is that we are now officially in the advent season, the season of Christmas. While we often associate this season with the personal attitudes of joy and peace, we usually don't stop to ask about how people in general, but Christians in particular, are expected to find this peace and this joy. The answer I believe is that joy and peace arise from the virtue of hope. For example, Romans 15:13 (RSV) encourages us saying, "May the God of *hope* fill you with all joy and peace." In short, Christmas is really all about hope!

Finally, however, it seems to me that we need to talk about hope because right now is a season when hope is much needed. With Thanksgiving behind us, many of us, students and faculty alike, are beginning to realize how much must be done before Christmas. The pressure of papers, exams, and grading is suddenly very real. Some of you may be pretty discouraged about all this. You may be wondering if you can possibly make it through.

You may be wondering if you even belong here and whether you should return next spring. For you, the picture may at times seem quite hopeless. So, it makes sense for us to think together about hope.

Prayer...

> May the words of my mouth and the meditations of our hearts be acceptable in Thy sight, Oh Lord, our Strength and our Redeemer!

Two weeks ago yesterday my wife Ellen and I left with twelve college trustees and travel partners for Africa. Among other things we visited some of your friends studying at Greenville's program in Mozambique. They are doing well and look forward to seeing you here on campus in a week or two. Africa is a continent that encourages one to become a person of hope. That morning two weeks ago, we approached the Delta Airlines counter in Atlanta and presented our tickets and passports. The agent looked them over and then responded calmly that "Ellen will not be traveling today." "Excuse me?!" I said! "She will not be travelling because she does not have the three empty pages in her passport required for visas to enter South Africa." When I showed him three empty pages, he responded pleasantly that they did not have the word "*Visas*" printed in faint blue letters at the top, so while the rest of us flew all night to Africa, Ellen would need to fly to New York City alone and obtain stapled additional pages in her passport. First, for a few moments I *hoped* he was kidding. Then, I looked at his eyes and *hoped* he would take pity. Then I just *hoped* he would let me talk to someone else behind security! When he did, I *hoped* the South African Airline agent would call Johannesburg and *hoped* they would accept my wife's evidence of an ongoing charter flight as proof she really did not intend or even want to stay in their country more than overnight in transit. That call didn't happen! Instead, if she was to board our flight at all, she would not be allowed to exit the airport in Joburg for our overnight, but instead must continue onward ahead of and independent of our group. So as proof of her transit status, I was forced to buy a single one way ongoing ticket for her alone to a small city outside South Africa that she had never visited and that was not on our itinerary.

Then I *hoped* our travel agent might be able to arrange to drive my wife six hours from that city up the recently war ravaged African coast of the Indian Ocean to join us a day or two later. That's a *lot* of *hoping*!!

All through the twenty-hour transatlantic flight that night Ellen and I hoped those arrangements were being made. When we arrived in Johannesburg, we decided at least to try approaching South African immigration, we *hoped* and *hoped* and *hoped* that by waiting to be last in line and picking the friendliest appearing agent, Ellen would be allowed to stay with our group. Hallelujah! The lack of empty pages turned out to be no problem— and now we are just *hoping* that we get a refund on that expensive ticket to a strange city in a far-off country.

Of course, there are far more profound and sobering ways in which Africa forces one to consider hope. Our conversations last week with my friends in Zimbabwe about the ongoing meltdown of their economy, the progressive erosion of the rule of law, the fading of the free press, the precipitous drop in life expectancy due to AIDS, and the unimaginable emigration of the strongest and brightest among their fellow citizens, are just a few realities that force them and force us all to consider hope. I could go on with many other stories from just the last two weeks; not the least of which would be the image I carry of the four-year-old girl with a red plastic cup and tattered dress, begging me for a penny or two while pulling her blind father along beside her. But the bottom line is that Africa encourages—maybe even requires—a person to think about hope!!

What is hope? Hope it seems is a desire or a need we have which we hold with an optimistic expectation of attaining it! "I hope we win!" In other words, I want to win, and I'm optimistic we will. "I hope she comes!" In other words, I want her to come, and I'm optimistic she will! "I hope I pass!" In other words, I want to pass, and I'm optimistic I will.

So, the first obvious element of hope is to want something. This means there must be a need or a goal—something desirable is lacking! Hope makes no sense if we have everything we want and need. If you did not need to pass those exams next week or turn in that paper this week to graduate, then you could not really be said to "Hope that you pass them!"

If my wife Ellen did not need relief from pain caused by her cancer then I could not begin to hope that our appointment in St. Louis tomorrow will bring good reports from her doctor!

Until we have such desire; until we have such need, there can be no hope. Regarding our hope for salvation, Oswald Chambers puts it this way in his devotional for this morning. "Conviction of sin always brings a fearful binding sense of the law, it makes a man [or a woman] *hopeless*" (*My Utmost,* 12/1)! My student and faculty friends, if you are like me this morning, it is easy at times like these to know only my need, only my own inadequacy, only my inability to do what it seems I must do. If that is all we know, then we are men and women without hope. Merely wanting, merely needing, without expectation is at best mere wishful thinking, or at worst resignation and even hopelessness!

But this brings us to the second, and what I think is the most interesting, part about hope; the "attitude" part. The expectation, the optimism, that what we hope will come to pass. So, if hope is a virtue of character then we should strive to cultivate this attitude; i.e., how do we get this attitude? Let me suggest the attitude involves two parts: an *outside* part and an *inside* part.

The *outside* part of hope has to do with what we know about the thing hoped for. For example, the more I know about South African immigration law, or about Delta Airlines policies, or about the subject of my course, or even about the nature of cancer, the easier it is for me to judge whether I can hope about these things! This is of course why we often hear it said, especially among the underprivileged, that education is a key to hope. Knowledge can provide the *outside* part of creating the expectant, optimistic attitude that makes hope hopeful!

Consider for example our hope for meaning or hope for everlasting life. To some extent, our knowledge of the world, based on experience and thought, can help us to be hopeful. Romans tells us that nature is such that every person has enough evidence of God's presence to be able to hope for everlasting life.

But unfortunately, sometimes our knowledge is inadequate. Or perhaps what knowledge we do have gives us no reason to be expectant and optimistic. How then can there be hope? Perhaps I don't know much South African law, or much about the course material, or much about cancer. Perhaps we know too much about the law or about cancer. Perhaps I am not a scientist or philosopher who can see very much of God's hand at work in the world. What then?

In such cases there can still be hope if we know something about the persons who control these circumstances. If only we knew the Delta agent personally, or even what he had for breakfast. If only we knew that smiling South African immigration officer or what her family was like. Or if only we knew Dr. Weilbacher, and her educational and research experience. If we knew these people, it would be much easier to have hope—in spite of our own knowledge and understanding.

Consider for example how our knowledge of God and his love for the world can give us hope even if our knowledge of this world is limited and inadequate. A personal relationship with the one who controls this world, gives us the knowledge we need to be people of Hope! As Oswald Chambers puts it:

> Think Who the New Testament says that Jesus Christ is, and then think of the despicable meanness of the miserable faith we have…. I haven't had this and that experience! Think what faith in Jesus Christ claims…then stand in implicit adoring faith in Him (*My Utmost*, 11/13).

But once again a barrier arises. What if we don't know about these people? What if we don't believe we know about God? In other words, what if our knowledge is just too limited. Can we ever expect to have hope? Can we ever hope to hope?

This brings us to what I like to call the *inside* part of hope. Like so many other virtues; like so many other aspects of character, hope often comes down to a decision. It often comes down to a choice. My decision often makes the difference. I choose to hope about the Delta agent. I choose to hope about the Johannesburg immigration lady. I choose to hope about my wife's doctor. Sometimes we call this *inside* part of hope, trust. In fact, the dictionary tells us that the word *hope* is often used synonymously with *trust* and to trust is surely a decision we make.

The American pragmatist, William James, was convinced that sometimes, when our knowledge is insufficient, truth can only be realized by choosing. Trapped on a cliff where the only escape is by a leap, without knowledge that we can succeed, we can realize the truth of that hope only by choosing it.

To become people of hope then, we must recognize our *need*— sometimes our desperate need—then seek to *know* all we can about the particulars of our hope, learn all we can about the person who controls the circumstances, and ultimately make *decisions*, make choices to trust. Paradoxically, hope requires what are often seen as contrasting actions: Knowing and Choosing.

The application of this principle to hope about immigration, hope about exams and papers, is clear. Our ability to hope depends on our choices, on our decisions. These are not matters of mere feeling. Hope need not be limited by our feelings of discouragement, or by our circumstances or personal inadequacies. Hope even in the simplest things will depend on what we decide.

But how does this apply to our hope for peace, for joy, or for meaning in life? Or how does it apply to hope for eternity? In a nutshell, it seems to me that the inadequacy of our own ability to know the God of our universe forces us to decide whether to choose simply to trust Him. If we are unwilling to contribute this *inside* part of hope, if we are unwilling to take this step, we are unable to have hope. If on the other hand we give up the control of our lives, the ambitions and goals we have, even the need to know, and instead choose surrender to Christ, we become people of hope.

It is obvious that the validity of any hope found in this way then depends on the trustworthiness and reliability of the one in whom we choose to trust. It is central to the hope of those who follow Jesus Christ that he is utterly trustworthy. He is the same yesterday, today, and forever. But of course, one can never have that hope unless you bring the *inside* part, the choice. If you are feeling hopeless today, I invite you to make a decision now. Bring that *inside* part to hope. Choose to place your hope in Christ and share that decision with a friend.

One final word. I have found the evidence of hope in my life is always a surprising, amazing sense of profound peace and joy even in the midst of crisis. I pray you will feel that amazement this Christmas season as I do this very day.

FOURTEEN

PATIENCE: "SPRINTING"

JANUARY 26, 2005

As always, it is good to see you back! For those that were here for Interterm I hope you have had a refreshing pause this past weekend. And for those who have been away since before Christmas, we are especially glad to see you back home with us again! Some of you were off campus last fall; in Oxford or Africa where I got to see you in November. You will really add to us this spring as "salt & light" among us. And finally, some of you are brand new! I won't embarrass you by making you stand, but I hope you feel a warm welcome. Most of us that work at Greenville College do so because we love students. When you're away we miss you!

Over the past year or two, I have shifted in my chapel talks from focusing on paradoxes to talking about some of the virtues that we have in mind when we say Greenville College tries to help educate you for lives of character. In the past months I have spoken about the virtues of courage, hope, faith, honesty, responsibility, and discipline.

Virtues are those qualities of your character that make you tend to behave in good ways, especially when you are under pressure. Vices of course are the opposite. They are qualities of our character that make us tend to behave in bad ways, again especially under pressure. Most of us can choose to do the right things when we have time to think about it. But the real test of character is what we do by "instinct," by "character," when push comes to shove under the pressure of time, or stress, or peer influence.

Character is not about what you have in your head, it's about what you have trained yourself to be like in your intellectual, moral, and spiritual "reflexes." In fact, character is a lot like the reflexes of a trained athlete who when the ball comes at a certain speed at a certain angle, almost automatically moves in ways that have been practiced over and over. It's like the reaction you have riding a bicycle or driving a car when the handlebars or wheel move a little one way or the other. You lean or turn almost automatically. It's like the reaction I learned after many bungled landings in a small plane. As the plane settles twenty feet off the ground, you feel it in the "seat of your pants," and manage the throttle, yoke, and pedals automatically. There is little thought given to it because those "reflexes" have been honed by practice over long periods of time. If we hope to help you become persons of character, it will not happen just by our talking about them like I want to do today. You must find and take every opportunity—we must help you!—to practice them over and over!

Most of you have heard me say that intellectual, moral, and spiritual growth, like physical development, requires stretching, or when I say it more directly, "pain." But now I am reminding you that besides pain, this growth, whether physical, intellectual, moral, or spiritual also requires practice. To that old familiar saying, "No pain, no gain!" I am adding the equally familiar, and thus equally easily overlooked saying, "Practice makes perfect."

Today I want to talk to you about the virtue of patience for two reasons. First, because it is a virtue all by itself. It is a quality of character, that makes us better people inside all by itself. But second, it also happens to be the virtue that helps us acquire *other* virtues. It does this by allowing us to persist in whatever practices are essential to acquiring any virtue. In other words, it is both a virtue in itself, and it is a "helper" virtue too.

Before I go any farther, I must confess two doubts that I had over the weekend as I thought about speaking to you today. First, I couldn't help seeing that talking about patience to young people might be a lot like spitting into the wind. When I was younger, waiting was the last thing I wanted to do. I wanted everything yesterday! But as you will see, it seemed the Lord used circumstances to keep nudging me toward the topic. My second doubt arose because I am still one of the most impatient people I know! Just ask my wife Ellen or my assistant Tamie sitting down there right now. How can someone as impatient as I am, give anyone help on patience! But I found some consolation and courage to go ahead when I read one church father, Tertullian, confess to the same failing ("Of Patience")! He remarks that it's no worse for an impatient person to speak of patience, than for a sick person to speak of health. In both cases it is a virtue of which the person has scant supply but great desire! So, with that background and those caveats, I'd like to say a few things about *Patience: "Sprinting."*

Prayer...

> May the words of my mouth and the meditations of our
> hearts be acceptable in Thy sight, Oh Lord, our Strength
> and our Redeemer!

We live in a day of instant gratification! In our culture, waiting seems to be the surest sign of powerlessness! The rich and famous never wait. Imagine President Bush waiting for Marine One or for Air Force One. Imagine Michael Jackson waiting for someone to bring him an umbrella for the sun! And more and more we do everything we can to make sure we don't wait either. Regular mail is called "snail mail" so nowadays a huge percentage of quite ordinary business mail goes "Express Mail" or "Overnight" at great expense and for no obvious reason! Most of the time even that is too slow, so we use fax or email. But more and more even email is too slow. How many of you use "instant messaging" on your computers? How many of you use "text messaging" because you can't even wait until your friend is at their computer to get the instant message?! For those unwilling to wait in line for their rental car, Hertz has the #1 Club, Avis has the Wizard Club, National has the Emerald Club, Budget has the Fastbreak Club—you get the idea! Microwaves and MacDonald's spare us having to wait to eat, while VCRs and DVRs spare us having to adjust our schedule to that of cable TV. [*Update* 2020: *Today few even bother to "record" shows but stream them off "On Demand" services.*] Even wealthy celebrities shoplift because they don't want to wait! And then there's the ubiquitous cell phone. On the freeway in California a week ago, I counted more than half the drivers talking on their phones—and those were just the ones without headsets or built-ins! As I walked through the terminal in Orange County, everyone was talking, but to no one around them! In airports when I see the rare person talking on a pay phone I now find myself wondering why! "What's wrong?!" "Did they lose their cell phone?" Phones ring in all the wrong places—concerts, churches, chapel, and worst of all, even in classrooms! (I'm sure that never happens here!) We just can't wait to share urgent information like "We'll see you at the baggage claim in two minutes!" or "I finally decided to wear the red sweater today." or "The sun actually rose as we expected!"

In fact, cell phones are a big part of why I wanted to talk to you about patience today. Last week, in California, my cell phone suddenly decided to get sick. I say sick not dead because my email on the phone worked fine, the phone web access worked fine, even the instant messaging and text messaging worked fine. But with four bars of signal, whenever I tried to place a call, the signal faded and I got that horrible message, "Searching for Network!" Believe it or not, I simply couldn't place any call at all! When Ellen and I emerged from a visit to the home of the owner of In-N-Out Burgers, I tried to call my daughter to tell her to use the GPS and come pick us up as soon as possible. No luck! We finally had to resort to going back in the house to use the land line! Then because of our delay we had to walk two blocks on foot and wait at least a full fifteen minutes to be picked up. Why it was positively embarrassing!

So back in St. Louis this weekend, I sprinted (sic!) for the nearest Sprint store where I had a lot of time and material to help me think about patience. Friday night I was greeted by the Sprint host at the Richmond Heights store on Clayton Road and took my place with the congregation in the chairs waiting for my name to be called. It was an hour and a half lesson on patience. I say "on" patience, not "in" patience because—for once—I wasn't the impatient one. I had no place else to go that night; Ellen was in the hospital. But more on that later. I saw six to eight Sprint representatives behind counters dealing with irate customers one after the other. It was exhausting. One woman shouted about the refund of $20 that she said the agent had promised her; apparently on an earlier visit in the presence of the woman's daughter. She accused the young man of lying and racism in such a loud voice that the "bouncer"—yes there are "bouncers" in Sprint stores these days—slowly and inconspicuously moved himself to her side of the store, while five to six of us watched from our ringside seats. Another young woman at a different window raised her voice and eventually stalked out, only to return a few minutes later with some "higher up" on the phone who, "Wants to talk with you, you lousy Sprint agent!" You could feel the tension in the air, and I felt my stomach tightening up just listening! Amazed at the show, and never one to pass up an audience, I remarked out loud to the receptionist and all the others within earshot still waiting with me, that Sprint needed to provide a big tub of TUMS [antacids] for the spectators in the evening's entertainment. The receptionist guy replied, asking if I'd had a good day. I said "Yes," this wasn't bothering me, because compared to the fact I'd just admitted my wife to Barnes Hospital, it was pretty trivial whether my phone worked. He said it had been a bad day for him. I could see why. I was tense just listening in for ninety minutes! Those agents must have some amazing training in patience to deal with it for eight hours! Talk about impatience for a phone replacement; one earlier customer had even stolen the receptionist's own phone! When I was called to the counter a few minutes later the young man apologized for the furor. It saddened me to hear him say in a kind of stunned hurt voice regarding the first shouting woman, "I've never been talked to that way before in my life!" This was about $20!

I left Sprint that night still without a working phone, and had to go to a different store the next day where I spent another two and a half hours; this time without quite so much melodrama! Six hours later, on the second day my cell phone issues were resolved. Now you might suppose I had been a paragon of patience. But it all took its toll—insidiously. When added to hospital delays that had me sleeping overnight in my wife's room, involved multiple phone calls to doctors, constant prodding of nurses to start a lifesaving IV drip, to bring water or clean up vomit, and twelve hours added unnecessarily to our visit because the clerk scheduling MRIs was unwilling to use common sense! You get the picture! It all left me too well aware how frazzled we all get, and how easily impatience builds up almost unobserved and eventually blows our heads off! Road rage doesn't come from being cut off in traffic. It comes from the lurking, lingering hostility and anger that erupt when impatience bursts the bonds of our character and spews poison into the lives of everyone around us including our own souls!

Patience...

So, what is patience? The word comes from the Latin word "pati" for suffering. In fact, we sometimes use the word "suffer" interchangeably with patience. "The toddler mauled the long-*suffering* family Labrador!" Patience is "the capacity [virtue] to tolerate delay, trouble, or suffering without becoming angry or upset" (*Compact OED*). It means bearing pain or trials calmly without complaint, showing restraint under provocation, remaining steadfast despite opposition, difficulty, or adversity (*Merriam Webster Online*). St. Augustine says it is "That by which we tolerate evil things with an even mind" ("*On Patience*").

Often, we understand things better by looking at their opposite. Tertullian says that *impatience* is such a deep and pervasive vice that it might actually be considered, if not the root of all evil then, at least the accomplice or accessory of all evil. To use the language of chemistry, he seems to be saying impatience is like a *catalyst* for evil. Catalysts are not themselves part of the reaction but serve to accelerate reactions that would take place not at all or at least much more slowly without the catalyst. In other words, impatience catalyzes vice. Gluttony is impatient hunger. Gossip is impatient curiosity. Slander is hasty judgment, impatient to find the facts. Adultery is impatient lust—unwilling to wait for sexual satisfaction through marriage. Idolatry, like that of Israel while Moses was on the mountain, is perhaps a form of impatient worship. Do we wait for the Spirit patiently in our frantically scheduled worship services? Was the problem in Eden really impatient dominion?

In an interesting comment on the effects of impatience, Augustine remarks that while the impatient person will not "suffer" (tolerate) the evil of waiting, they will instead "suffer" (bear) the far greater evil within their souls that comes from its selfish haste! Impatience is shortsighted.

But where do we see impatience in our lives? Where do you and I really need patience? Let me suggest some places. If the shoe fits, wear it! If you have ears to hear, listen!

There are lots of *small* areas where we need patience. I say "small" because on the one hand these are fairly trivial inconsequential areas of our lives. But on the other hand, they are absolutely crucial! As I have already said we learn all virtues by constant practice. That practice can come in any part of our behavior no matter how big or small. Patient repetitive small exercises of any virtue make it grow. So patient small exercises of patience are crucial too. As the saying goes, "Character is formed *not* in the big decisions of life, but in the thousands of little ones." If you don't remember anything else this morning, I hope you'll leave thinking about the little things you do every day, every hour, every moment, that shape your character—and especially the virtue of patience.

Small things—like whether you are irritated standing in line handing in your chapel card, in line for lunch, in line at registration, in line at the store, in line at the traffic light. If you're like me, you switch to a faster lane on the freeway or in the grocery store and it automatically slows down! Sometimes I'm convinced God has a "special agent in charge" of teaching Jim Mannoia patience. The angel follows me around slowing down lines and lanes just to foil my efficiency schemes and offering me instead a chance to learn patience! Did you ever feel that way? Maybe you are irritated by your roommate; they never seem to change, no matter how many gentle—or not so gentle—hints you give them about lights, loud bad music, borrowed clothes, dirty dishes, long phone calls at night, or just plain messiness. Or maybe it's the faculty member that doesn't return your paper soon enough. Now you may think I'm saying the fault is always yours and that roommates, professors, checkout clerks, and other drivers don't need to be improved. Not so! More on that in a minute. But for now, I'm just saying that no matter whether there is a real need for improvement in others, there is always opportunity for us to learn patience. Maybe if we spent more time figuring out how we could benefit from others' weaknesses and mistakes, we'd be better able to help them and ourselves all at once.

But there are also *big* things in which we need patience. Some of you are seniors and you're worried about what happens when you graduate. It's tempting to suppose it will never happen. My future son-in-law, Brandon, just got a job last week. He was relieved, because for three months he wondered and worried! We worry and worry and worry. I remember when I was in third grade, I was terrified one day when I saw some eighth graders fighting with one another. I went home crying saying I was afraid of growing up. I'll never forget my dad taking me on his lap and holding up my little hand, palm to palm flat against his big hand with fingers splayed apart. He said, "Jimmy, don't worry, you still have this many years till you are in eighth grade. (That's the only reason I know I must have been in third!) By the time you get to their age, you'll be ready!" He was saying, take each step as it comes; "Be patient."

But this same principle of patience applies to other big things. It means we must be careful about impatience regarding all aspects of our own personal development. You may not yet know how to be a really good friend. Give it time. You may be impatient with some of the hard lessons you are learning in the classroom. They may be stretching you more than you can understand. You want to see right now how it will help you get a job or how it will make you a better person. Have you ever asked yourself or a "prof" how a particular topic is "relevant" to the job you have in mind? Have you ever asked how doubts and challenges to your faith could possibly make you a stronger Christian? Again, I am not saying there is no need for improvement in how these kinds of "trying experiences" are delivered; there always is. But I am saying we need patience over years to see the effect of this equipping and shaping educational process. I always enjoy the reports from GC alums five to ten years out who do see what patience has wrought in their lives.

Finally, for some reason I feel the need to mention one final big area in which we need patience. It is in regard to our own self-esteem. I know there are many in this room who don't feel they are worth very much. You may even want to give up; on college, on relationships, even on life. I think your parents and others that love you would want to remind you of what I have wanted my children to remember. You've seen the T-shirt, "I may not be perfect, but parts of me are excellent—and God isn't finished with me yet!" I urge you to be patient with yourself. Don't act rashly. Don't give up on yourself. Remember God is *still* at work.

Barriers to Patience...

Before we finish, let me turn to what I think are two barriers to patience in our lives. First, as I hinted a few moments ago, is the barrier of knowing *when* to be patient and when, instead, to press harder for improvement either of our own circumstances or of the system that is trying our patience. One response I often find in myself is the temptation to respond impatiently because I don't think I should be walked on! It's un-American for anyone to take advantage of me. I need to speak up and press for my rights. Often impatience is rooted in this rationale. Well yes, sometimes we must speak up. This is especially true in cases of genuine abuse. But in our impatient, rights oriented culture, it is important to remember that people constantly took advantage of Christ. Are we patient enough to allow the circumstances, however unjust they may feel, to do the work of building character in us? Remember patience is a helper virtue to all other virtues, just as impatience is a catalyst for most vices!

Another frequent rationale for impatience is that we fool ourselves into thinking we are just unselfishly trying to improve the system. How often I hear students and employees say, "Oh, I'm pushing the issue not for *my* sake, but for the benefit of others who come after. I don't want this to happen to them." I confess, I often hear *myself* say the same thing! Ok! Good point! Without some who are bold we never make progress. The challenge then is to know when to press forward impatiently and when to hold back. This is surely one of those complex, paradoxical grey, slippery slope judgments in life for which there is no easy answer. But let me suggest that one important consideration is our motive for impatience. If it is to bring justice or help to *another*, it may be right. If it is for *personal* gain or *personal* revenge, then think very carefully about the lost opportunities for growth in patience before pushing ahead.

A second barrier to developing the virtue of patience in our life is not just the challenge of knowing *when* to exercise it, but also of knowing *how* to exercise it. I am afraid that too many of us think that patience requires us to cover up our real feelings on and on almost indefinitely. When it sometimes eventually becomes obvious this is impossible, we blow our stack, completely out of control. This tendency may be particularly common among Christians because we seem to believe that confrontation or showing displeasure is unchristian. What I think is missing, is the ability—a skill that is natural for some but that I think can also be acquired—to show our feelings, express our impatience, more gradually. This often prevents the blowout, and sometimes accomplishes our goal more quickly than either the cover-up or the blowout would do. People cannot respond if they don't know how you feel; but they also balk at responding if you blow your top. In short it may be that we need to learn to be gradually *assertive* without becoming *aggressive*. Mull over that distinction in your mind and consider where you stand along that scale.

I have said that patience is both a virtue in itself, and a helper virtue that enables us to persist in the practices essential for the formation of any virtue. These twin values, one intrinsic and the other instrumental, are *both* affirmed over and over in the Bible.

Galatians tells us that patience is a "fruit of the Spirit" (Galatians 5:22). In other words, when the Holy Spirit is alive in us, we will show His presence through the patience of our behavior and our attitudes. Like the fruit and flower of a plant, it is good in and of itself. So likewise, in your character; it is a beautiful thing in God's eyes to see a patient person.

But the Bible also underscores the second twin value; that patience is an instrument to achieve other good things in our lives. It is an impression of this "helper" role that I most want to leave with you today. Romans 5 (vv. 3–5) urges us actually to rejoice in our difficulties because when faced patiently, they produce character, and that character in turn produces hope. When I talked to you in December I begged you to remember that as followers of Jesus Christ we ought always, and above all others, to be people of hope. Our hope is a hope that "does not disappoint us because God's love has been poured into our hearts" (Romans 5:5 RSV). If you take your walk with Christ seriously, and genuinely want to be a person of hope, expect difficulties, but then be sure to face them patiently. Otherwise, you will miss the lesson in character that the Holy Spirit wants you to learn. Sometimes I pray, "Lord, help me to learn my hard lessons quickly and remember them, so you don't have to keep stretching me over and over to learn them or repeating the pain again and again for me to relearn them!" Lest this sound like a recipe for self-torture, remember that James (1:12) tells us that the man is happy who endures difficulties *patiently!*

In closing please consider my favorite passages regarding patience. They come from Hebrews (6:11). There we are urged to be "earnest" Christians; that is really serious about achieving the hope we have. To do this we are told not to be "sluggish" Christians, "slackers" in our attitudes. But instead, we are to be "energetic" (keen) in following the example of others who, as the Phillips version puts it, "through sheer patient faith, come to possess the promise" (6:12). Notice this is about our attitude not our behavior. Get the attitude and everything else follows!

But above all be patient. I recall in 1970, being in a relationship I eagerly wanted to see go forward. I can remember it seemed to stall and stall and stall. I agonized, believing that unless I figured it out, unless it moved forward, I must not yet have found God's will. I remember to this day, the liberation I felt when that friend sent me the passage from Hebrews 10:36 (Phillips). "Patient endurance is what you need, if, *after doing God's will*, you are to receive what he has promised." It doesn't say, first be patient then you will see His will. Rather it assures us that we may well already have done His will, may well be doing His will, and yet nevertheless may well still have to endure patiently in order to receive the joy and peace he has promised and for which we hope. God's promise is to transform us into the image of His Son Jesus Christ. Today I urge you, please, please, please, "Be Patient."

Let's pray: *Lord, in the quiet of this moment, on the cusp of a new semester, teach us to be patient. Amen.*

FIFTEEN

JOY AND GRIEF: A PARADOXICAL SEASON

As is my usual custom, I want to talk today about paradox and about virtue. I talk about paradox a lot because I believe it is central to liberal arts education. Students of the liberal arts recognize that the most important issues in life are usually not as simple as they first seem. They are not simple because as Scripture tells us, in this life we "see through a glass darkly," and only one day will it be "face to face" (1 Corinthians 13:12 KJV). In other words, the means we have for knowing truth in this life are always limited. So, we must learn to accept ambiguity, while still holding to our convictions. That is very hard to do. It requires both real humility and real passion at the same time. That is paradoxical. I call it critical commitment.

But I also talk a lot about virtue. That's because at Greenville we educate for character, and character is just exactly the collection of our virtues. It's not enough to have great skill for nuancing in our mind those important yet paradoxical issues of life. If we fail to act despite their ambiguity, we are, to use C.S. Lewis's turn of phrase, "men without chests" (*Abolition of Man*). Winston Churchill spoke of politicians paralyzed by conflicting pressures in the face of Hitler's atrocities. He believed they would only remain emphatically and intentionally undecided. So, paradoxically, they were strongly committed to be uncommitted. In more contemporary terms, these are people like those in the current TV advertisements for the Royal Bank of Scotland, who stand trapped in a broken aerial gondola or sit at a table next to a choking colleague theorizing about what ought to be done, but failing to act. When the hero steps forward, the conclusion is simple, "Less talk, more action."

So, when the question of what to talk about today arose in my mind I knew it would be about paradox and virtue. But which paradox and which virtue? Wednesday night at the GCSA Christmas Around the World event—with great food by the way—I asked a couple of student friends what they thought I should say. I had been thinking about speaking on the virtue of joy. Hannah (Hawksbee) said that sounded good but given the events of my year, I was probably in a good position to talk about finding hope in the face of grief. Stephanie (Plant) and Scott (Humpherys) said it didn't matter what I talked about so long as I just told good stories! So, I started searching my frequently defective mental hard disk for paradoxical Christmas stories!

I remembered the story I had told students right here six years ago illustrating the need to trust. But none of you was here then and the story had many lessons for me. So, let me tell it again. It was late December of 1968, almost forty years ago, I left Boston in a snowstorm headed for Christmas to visit my parents who were missionaries in Brazil. I had sweat all summer on a highway construction gang in Lansing, Michigan, to earn just enough money for this once a year two week visit with my family. I was loaded with all kinds of special supplies and gifts—most of them the kind you could not purchase in Brazil in those days. As misfortune would have it, because of a blizzard in Boston, and despite running through the Miami airport with those heavy packages, I arrived at my connecting gate to see the plane for Brazil pulling away. Never mind that it sat for forty-five minutes within sight on the runway. I was stranded. And because I had chosen Brand X, a sketchy South American airline, which would not transfer my ticket to anyone else, I was stuck in Miami for three days. The good news was that in that century, the airlines actually cared enough to put me up and feed me for those days. It was Twinkies and hot dogs in the Starlight Motel, but it beat the airport or the street and there was nothing I could do. To pass the time, I bought and read a New York Times bestseller late into the night in that dark creaky room. It was Rosemary's Baby, the story of the birth of the devil through an immaculate conception! Bad choice! It "scared me to death."

During the day however, I walked the streets and on the last day visited a local store to buy some lime Jell-O for my mom—a holiday essential unavailable in São Paulo. As I was returning to the motel through a residential neighborhood, wearing torn blue jeans, scruffy sideburns, and very long hair, a patrol car pulled alongside, and the officer got out to question me. He said several residents had called in stating I was too old to be walking rather than driving in that neighborhood. (Hmmm!) The policeman asked where I was staying. I said, "In the Starlight Motel." When he asked why, I said, "I'm leaving for Brazil tomorrow." When he asked what I had in the small brown bag, I said "Lime Jell-O for my mother." In retrospect those weren't smart answers I guess! He took my student ID card, and while I kissed the hood of his car for a few minutes, he discovered there had been an "all-points bulletin" for someone from M.I.T. who was thought to be in Miami and was wanted back in Boston for murder. Ouch! Again, not good! I spent the next three hours locked in the back of his car while Miami's finest did his normal patrol waiting for a radio report answer back from Washington, D.C., on a V. James Mannoia. The ride was of course fine with me since I had nothing else to do anyway but go back and scare myself to death reading. I learned a lot about police work in sketchy neighborhoods that afternoon. The radio report on me never came. But he dropped me off at the Starlight, with good wishes for a great holiday with my folks. He said, he knew more about me by talking for three hours than the report could have told him anyway! Nice guy!

This story reminds me that Christmas is a paradoxical season. It is a time often of very mixed feelings. It embraces the apparently opposing even paradoxical qualities of joy and grief. That paradox is what I want to talk about today.

I know this may make me sound like the Grinch. That's because most of us think of Christmas as the one occasion each year that represents unqualified, unpolluted goodness. Isn't it all about love, joy, peace, and hope? But even my brief December arrest in Miami makes it clear Christmas is not simple. I was full of joy at the prospect of reunion with my family for the first time in a year, having no communication except letters for all that time. I was full of joy knowing I'd left "blizzardy" Boston to spend the holiday with those I loved, in warm weather, on the beaches of Guarujá. But even before I could arrive, I was already filled with fear; and I don't mean just about Rosemary's Baby! I feared I'd end up in jail with no one even knowing where I was. Keep in mind this is pre-cell phones, pre-text messages, and even pre-phones of any kind in our home in Brazil. What's more, even before arriving home I was already full of fear of saying goodbye to my family for another whole year after Christmas and fear of the awful first semester examinations I would have to take back in frigid Boston in January, only hours after leaving those warm beaches. So, I could hardly feel the joy, for all the anticipated grief. It was a time of hugely mixed feelings. You may be facing a Christmas of paradox, a Christmas of hugely mixed feelings too. And of course, this Christmas is certainly one of mixed feelings for me. It is full of grief from losing my wife Ellen six months ago, yet full of joy about the prospects for a new future ahead.

"Joy and Grief." That was the title of the story on CNN last Thursday morning as I exercised. The picture showed Andrue Smith, a twenty-eight-year-old construction worker in Tucson, holding his brand-new triplets—all boys! He calls them "Daddy's little army." His joy was obvious, as he said, "All I wanted was a son." He got three for Christmas. But his joy was matched by grief. After delivery, his wife Debbie's heart failed, her brain was damaged, and Andrue had to make the agonizing decision to end her life support. She will never see those boys. "I can't imagine a life without her," he said. Amazing joy mixed with amazing grief—all in the same Christmas season.

Grief...

Last week I read C.S. Lewis's book, *A Grief Observed.* In it Lewis recounts the agony of his grief from the loss of his wife Joy Davidman. Ironically, her name made his too a story of grief and Joy. Married only four years after a lifetime of bachelorhood, Lewis lost Joy to cancer. His grief took the form of deep doubts about God Himself. In early weeks, he railed at God, calling him the Cosmic Sadist, and even a divine Vivisector—killer of those who are still alive! (p. 44). He felt heaven's doors were bolted shut, and its windows dark. He felt abandoned. Prayer, he concluded, was nothing but "self-hypnosis." And in the end, the world turned "shabby," characterized by a "permanent provisional feeling" like just so many "cul-de-sacs" going nowhere and eventually slipping into "boredom tinged by nausea." Those feelings are not lost on me, and perhaps they are not lost on you even in this place and in this season.

Apparently, nineteen-year-old Robert Hawkins felt some of this grief in Omaha last week too. In the face of the joy of Christmas, he grieved his life, his years of therapy, his depression, and even his loss of work at McDonald's. He killed eight people, then himself. In the reopened mall on Saturday, one shopper, John Andrews, said, "It doesn't feel like a Christmas feeling." Then yesterday as I drove to Christmas carols at the

Botanical Garden in St. Louis I heard on the radio of another young man, this one twenty, shooting two others to death at a YWAM missionary training center in Arvada, Colorado. He's still on the loose. Literally the next story was how police at Loyola University in LA arrested a young college student for threatening to kill as many people as he could and hoping the police would then shoot and kill him. Two hours later, as I drove back to Greenville from the carols, there came yet another report of another young man shooting after the service at the New Life Church in Colorado Springs. A church security guard shot and killed him. This CNN story was entitled, "Faith and Fury." Talk about Christmas paradox.

What is this tragic grief? Grief it seems is the overwhelming pain born out of a terrible and irreversible loss of someone or something that was central to our very self-identity. As with Robert Hawkins, it can even be loss of our self. We are shattered. Existentialist Jean Paul Sartre echoes Lewis's allusion to "nausea" in his play of that same title. Sartre also echoes Lewis's "cul-de-sacs" in his play describing life as having "No Exit."

Maybe today you feel that loss of identity. Maybe you are feeling you are not the scholar or athlete or friend or even person you thought you were. The skill or relationship on which you have based your self-concept may be shattering. You may feel alone, discouraged, unloved, and even worthless. Maybe you even feel that terrible and seemingly irreversible emptiness. For you it may be a season of deep grief.

Joy...

In the face of such grief, what is joy, and where on earth is it? There's an old Sunday school song that says it's "down in my heart, up in my head, down in my feet." But it seems in short supply, even at Christmas. I remember days of terrible loneliness in college. Days when it seemed I didn't know who I was. Days when my identity as a member of a family so far away seemed lost. I remember that having a girlfriend seemed to drive those haunting feelings away for a while. But when they would break up with me—as seemed to happen over and over—I'd be devastated again, falling into grief. Each time I'd promise myself to remember that my identity was not in those relationships but in the one I had with my Father in heaven. As time would pass I'd find my balance and restore the joy of living, promising myself not to forget that deeper confidence. But only a few weeks would pass before yet another relationship would take my eyes off that deep confidence, and then that one too would be shattered leaving me to grieve again. I remember thinking how easily and foolishly I could change my focus from the solid substance of my relationship to Christ back to the mere "frosting" of relationships with others. It seemed I would never learn.

That's when I first began to understand that joy and happiness are quite different things altogether. Happiness, it seems, is something that depends on "happenings." Depending on what "happens" from day to day, or week to week, I might be happy or unhappy. These happenings included how well I did on an exam, how much pressure I felt in studies, whether I had a girlfriend, how well she treated me, and maybe even whether our crew team won its last race. Happiness was apparently like the waves on the top of the water, whipped up by every variable wind of the day. But joy on the other hand was the deep depth of relationship with Christ that stood underneath those happenings at all times. If the ocean is deep, the waves on the surface can rock and roll all they want but the depths remain calm. If, however, as seemed too often the case in my life back then, I did not have that depth of relationship with Christ, then whenever the waves grew large, the troughs of those ups and downs would scrape the bottom. And that was when I sometimes just wished life would end. It was a terrible grief. Maybe like me, you feel some of that today.

From Grief to Joy...

So how does one make a journey from grief to joy? Early last summer, shortly after Ellen died, I found myself without any appetite for many of the things I have always enjoyed most. I didn't want to eat good food. I didn't want to be with friends. I didn't want to drive fast. I didn't even want to take photographs—something I have done almost daily for over forty years. As I drove west in Ellen's Mini Cooper, passing gorgeous scenes, I wondered whether I would ever want to stop and take pictures again. But I remembered how so many friends had urged me not to act too soon.

"Don't make any decisions." "Let time pass." "Just put one foot ahead of the other." It was all good advice. In Hebrews we are told, "On the right path the limping foot recovers strength and does not collapse" (Hebrews 12:13 Phillips). On the right path! In other words, keep on keeping on.

So, I visited California and headed back east. By the time I got to Washington, D.C., I found myself taking pictures again—even from a speeding convertible in traffic! Continuing long-standing disciplines over enough time, choosing to remember the reality of my identity in Christ beneath the heavy seas of emotional happenings, is eventually bringing joy back to my life. As Lewis put it, in grieving his loss, he continued to take outside walks as much as he could. Then one day he realized "the face of nature was not emptied of its beauty and the world didn't look like a mean street" (*A Grief Observed*, p. 69). Soon amidst the tears there are twinkles (p. 88) because we have chosen by will, not emotion, to remember the joy that exists deep beneath the unhappiness of happenings.

You may ask what does this have to do with Christmas? It seems to me that Christmas also celebrates a paradoxical moment when grief and joy were mixed in large measure to form a turning point, a watershed moment in history. So, it can and should also be such a moment in our individual lives each year.

It was paradoxically a moment in history when God Himself experienced His deepest grief. His children had fallen away. His heart was broken. The part of His creation that was not just good but "very good," was deeply fallen. We cannot even imagine His grief. Our pain pales by comparison. Christmas represents the moment when God chose by an exercise of will to reach down in painful sacrifice, full of grief, to act. To squeeze His infinite Self into the form of a mere human was more painful than any of us could possibly imagine. To sacrifice His Son; what greater grief can a Father endure? We think of Christmas as all about a birth. But we must never forget that in reality it was also all about death. It is paradoxically about both.

Friday night at our annual alumni Christmas party at the home of Ken and Marjie Smith in St. Louis, we sang the familiar carol, "The First Noel." I had never noticed the line in one verse that reads, "By his blood mankind has bought." The First Noel, the Good News, is about a bloody painful grief filled sacrifice. In our reflection on the joy of this season let us never forget the paradox that such joy emerges out of grief by the divine act of will. The third advent candle, like the third candle of Lent, is pink, reminding us of the joy that emerges out of suffering.

That Joy is the confidence that lies below the surface of the happenings of this day, of this week, of this exam period, of this year, of this relationship, of this career, and even of this life. It is joy born of our confidence in Him alone, not our circumstances. It is joy that points us to a future that depends on Him not upon ourselves.

In Tucson this week, Andrue Smith received a gift of joy in the form of three new sons. But it arose out of his own grief-stricken act of will to end the life support for his wife.

In closing, hear these words of Scripture capturing the paradoxical nature of Christmas, one that embraces both grief and joy:

> But he took our suffering [grief] on him and felt our pain
> for us. We saw his suffering [grief] and thought God was
> punishing him. But he was wounded for the wrong we
> did; he was crushed for the evil we did. The punishment,
> which made us well, was given to him, and we are healed
> because of his wounds (Isaiah 53:4–6, New Century).

> Let Christ himself be your example as to what your
> attitude [choice] should be. For he, who had always been
> God by nature, did not cling to his prerogatives as God's
> equal, but stripped himself of all privilege by consenting
> to be a slave by nature and being born as mortal man.
> And, having become man, he humbled himself by living
> a life of utter obedience, even to the extent of dying,
> and the death he died was the death of a common
> criminal. That is why God has now lifted him so high,
> and has given him the name beyond all names, so that

at the name of Jesus "every knee shall bow", whether in Heaven or earth or under the earth. And that is why, in the end, "every tongue shall confess that Jesus Christ" is the Lord, to the glory of God the Father (Philippians 2:5–11, Phillips).

Have a blessed paradoxical Christmas full of joy arising out of grief.

SIXTEEN

LOYALTY AND COURAGE: LIONS, GORILLAS, AND HIPPOS

JANUARY 23, 2008

Good morning! I am home from three weeks in Africa. I arrived a couple days ago, and my body still thinks I'm eight hours ahead so I'm about ready for dinner. But it is good to be here.

I was in ten countries and visited eighteen different cities, a number of them for longer than I wanted. I bring you greetings from Keeley Scott in the Uganda Studies Program. She's doing well, having a great semester. I also bring you greetings from Justin, Chris, and Kelly who are with Go-ED and based in Kampala. They are also doing well, despite the challenges. It was ninety-five degrees there a couple days ago when I left and very humid to say the least. For those of you who know Professor Dwight Jackson, he sends warm regards as well. He is just as ornery as ever and that's a good thing when it comes to what he does directing *Food For the Hungry–Rwanda*.

I want to extend my welcome to new students. If you don't mind, would the new students that are here at Greenville for the first time this spring, raise your hands? We extend to you a "warm" Greenville welcome despite the twelve degree temperature as I walked here from Joy House this morning. Finally, I also want to extend a special welcome to the wife and family of Prof. Kurasha. Many of you have had courses from Dr. Kurasha, professor of philosophy and a colleague of mine for well over twenty years. His wife, also Dr. Kurasha, who is the Vice-Chancellor of the Open University in Zimbabwe, an institution with 19,000 students, has come to visit him here. I was with her and her daughter for a week in Harare just a few weeks ago and they beat me back here to Greenville. They are now staying with me in Joy House. Of course, many of you know Flora, their older daughter, a student here on campus, so I hope you will welcome with me Mrs. Dr. Kurasha and her youngest daughter Primrose. Would you both stand and be welcomed. They fed me well while I was in Harare and on the last evening there took me out to dinner which cost her $100 million dollars. Now, mind you it was Zimbabwe dollars, but it still took about a paper bag full of bills for us to pay that evening. I'll tell you more about that sometime if you'd like.

Let's bow our heads for a word of prayer.

> Lord, may the words of my mouth and the meditations of my heart, and our hearts, be acceptable in thy sight, Oh Lord, our strength and our redeemer. Amen.

Over the last few weeks, I've had plenty of time to read several books. One, given to me by a friend here at the college was called, *In a Pit, With a Lion, On a Snowy Day*. The book's very exciting and I encourage you to have a look. It's about Benaniah, who was one of King David's elite commandos, and the story was fascinating. In order to understand the context I looked at I Chronicles, chapters ten and eleven and read the details surrounding the story. It's about how King Saul had been killed, his son Jonathan had been killed, and David was the new king, moving from one victory to the next. He was in the middle of a successful period in his reign, just as you may be in the middle of a successful year. But he still faced another battle, perhaps even as you face a new semester. And perhaps like you, he was tired. In fact, the next battle was going to be with the Philistines who were encamped in his hometown of Bethlehem. He was in his "stronghold" near Jerusalem; the Philistines were encamped in Bethlehem. In short, though he was in a successful campaign, he was exhausted and wanted some relief. In particular, he was very thirsty, and the Philistines were standing between him and his home.

Maybe right now you have a little bit of that feeling. You'd like a little relief even though you've hardly begun. Maybe you too are even thinking of home? I suppose I could ask you; what is home for you this morning? Is it your family and perhaps literally where you were just last month at Christmas? Is home a friendship or relationship that means a great deal to you? Is home your health; maybe you are not well or someone you love is not well? Is home a job? Some of you seniors are beginning to think about what you're going to do in four months. Any of those things could be home for you. It could be something that you want and there could be something standing between you and your home. Until last summer, for thirty-five years, my wife Ellen was my "home." Today there is indeed a Philistine standing between me and my home, and that Philistine is the "philistine of death." It separates me from my home.

David had three mighty men: Abishai, a guy who had killed 300 of the enemy with his sword; another guy named Eleazar, and a man named Benaniah. These three mighty men were all both brave and loyal. Now, in the face of David's circumstances, his desire to be at home, thwarted by the Philistines, these three men loved David so much they made it their mission to get a drink of water for him from the well in his hometown. Benaniah was the son of Jehoidah, son of another valiant man. It says that Benaniah had killed two princes of Moab, which is pretty impressive because they were no doubt well-guarded. It also says he killed a twelve-foot-tall Egyptian. Now that must have been something to see! And, of course, as the name of the book suggests, Benaniah jumped into a pit with a lion on a snowy day and killed it. Mind you, he wasn't already in the pit; he wasn't fighting for his life, but for some strange reason he chose to go into that pit on a snowy day when one's footing would not be particularly good and presumably lions have "four-wheel drive." But he did it, and he slew the lion. He was a pretty impressive man to say the least. He was one of the three that made the trip to Bethlehem, to David's home; to overcome the Philistines, to bring David relief. They were brave and loyal men of David.

If you've been around Greenville very often, you know I talk a lot about character and service, and you know that I talk a lot about virtues and what the virtues might be that could make us men and women of character. Today I'd like to say a little bit about two of these. I also want to remind you that when I talk about Greenville College, I often talk about two guiding principles. One of them is the principle that we are a different kind of place because we are a *nurturing* place. A second reason why we are special and why we're different is because we're a *stretching* place. You often hear me say, "First, we want to be a place where you are nurtured and encouraged. But second, we also want to be a place where you are stretched."

Another way of putting this is to say that we are a community. Communities nurture. Communities are a place where you are encouraged. But good communities also try to push you out of your comfort zone. So, Greenville aspires to be a community that supports you but also pushes you out of your comfort zone; nurturing and stretching. Obviously, these are, in some ways, opposite principles that shape our community and make us unusual. We are both a *comfortable* place and, I hope, an *uncomfortable* place. Of course, the fact that these are opposites is why you also often hear me talk so much about *paradox* and how we have to embrace the paradoxes of life in order to grow personally.

So, nurturing and stretching make Greenville a place of opposites. And this contrast can be seen in the two virtues shown by Benaniah, Abishai, and Eleazar that day. I want to focus on bravery and loyalty, or to put them another way, on *courage* and *loyalty*.

Loyalty...

If you think about it, loyalty is a virtue of community. You can't be loyal all alone. Loyalty is what you find when people live in real community. It is part of what makes a community a place of nurture. David's friends were loyal, and they wanted to please him that day. They wanted to bring him relief; they wanted to bring him water from his home. When a person is loyal, they go out of their way, they go the extra mile, for those to whom they are loyal. When a person is loyal, he or she thinks the best of those others. If you have a friend that's loyal to you, they think the best of you, they always give you the benefit of the doubt. That's what it means to be loyal. That is the virtue of a community such as the kind I believe we are here at Greenville. So, I begin just by asking, "Are you a loyal friend? Are you willing to give your friends the benefit of the doubt? Are you willing to go the extra mile for them? Are you willing to think the best of them?"

Courage...

But the other virtue that Benaniah and his buddies showed that day is the virtue of courage. If loyalty is a virtue of a *nurturing* community, then courage is a virtue of *stretching*. Why? Because it takes courage to venture out of your comfort zone. It requires a moral effort of character to pull yourself up and to step out into something new. You've often heard me say, "No pain, no gain." If you aren't intentional about that, if we as an institution aren't intentional about that, then there's less likely to be growth, and we would certainly show very little courage. David's friends that day were brave. They stepped out of the comfort zone of David's stronghold and they marched, just three of them, against the forces of the Philistines and infiltrated them to get to the well outside of Bethlehem to bring their friend, out of loyalty, a bit of water from his home. They certainly illustrated courage that day by what they did.

But how do you illustrate courage? One of the ways in which you often hear me say we can get out of our comfort zone, and therefore show courage, is to be involved in cross-cultural experiences. As you can imagine, in the last few weeks I've seen your fellow students doing it and have had a little share myself!

A week ago, Monday I was standing at about 9,700 feet in the volcanic mountains on the northern border of Rwanda. In fact, in the course of the three hours I was hiking, I crossed over into the Democratic Republic of the Congo, perhaps several times without knowing it because there's no border post in the middle of the jungle. We were up there because we were tracking the silverback gorillas. For more than an hour I was among them, often within six to ten feet of perhaps the largest silverback gorilla in the world! This beast was nothing to be casual about. He was, according to reports, 250 kilos, which puts him at about 500 pounds. You could say that sitting in his presence took courage. But that was possible because there were other people around me; five other visitors, plus two guys who claimed to speak the gorilla's language, and two more with AK-47 machine guns. The main guide told me, "You know, if they begin to approach you, just back up slowly. If the young ones approach you quickly, back up quickly. If a juvenile approaches you quickly, just stand still because they only want to touch you." Right!!

So, I stood for ten minutes literally six feet from a 500 pound gorilla. He watched me as much as I watched him. In fact, I couldn't help but wonder, "Who's watching whom here?" He sat there in his nest; he looked at his fingernails, maybe he just had them manicured or something; he stuck one in his nose then looked over at me as if to say, "Whaddya lookin' at, buddy?" At one point, in order to show who was boss, he walked over to a twenty-five-foot tree that was five inches in diameter, grabbed it, and casually knocked it over. Two days before, one of the trackers that was with us had been with the same gorilla and the gorilla apparently decided he was just a little annoyed by this tracker who follows him twenty-four hours a day, seven days a week. So, he walked over to the tracker while everybody was standing watching, grabs him by the leg, drags him forty feet down the trail, drops him, and then casually comes back. Now, in some ways I kind of wish that had happened to me, because then wouldn't *that* have been a great story to tell you?! Or on the other hand, the day before we went out, the gorillas had urinated on another group from the trees. I thought, "Well, that would also be a story, but I would much rather have had it happen to Dwight Jackson standing next to me."

I'm not sure if it required courage to be out there. I felt at moments that I was behaving courageously, especially when there was an incredible crashing in the bush right in front of us and Dwight Jackson jumped straight up, came down, and I said, "Well Dwight has your heart stopped racing?" Or there was the moment when I was taking a picture and without my seeing her and without warning one of the large female gorillas strolled up from behind, then along beside me, about six inches from my left arm; she stopped about three feet ahead of me, and turned around and looked me in the eye as if to say, "Ok, what're *you* lookin' at?" I'm not sure visiting gorillas required courage, but I do know that cross-cultural experiences do!

During my trip I also visited the campus of Houghton College in Tanzania, a program which I had helped to develop about fifteen years ago. In order to get from one part of the campus to the other, you have to go across a deep rushing river, surrounded on both sides by high stone cliffs. The only way to do this is to use the zip line stretched across the gap. And oh, did I mention that the river is home to a large pod of hippos? (Mind you, more people are killed by hippos in Africa than by anything else, with the possible exception of the malaria mosquito.) Anyway, I had traversed the line during early evening to go across to the other side of campus for dinner. Afterwards, I had to return to my little visitor's hut, back across the river. But now it's pitch dark. You have to understand there's no electricity, and no light except a tiny little flashlight that I had stuck in my pocket and the battery was just about dead. So, I had to climb onto the zip line with a little pencil light which "no way" showed across the river to see where I was going to land, and let go to swing across, flying on the zip line into the pitch darkness towards a destination I couldn't see while I listened to the hippos underneath. My heart was racing a little faster than it normally would. Maybe that takes a certain kind of courage. It certainly took me out of my comfort zone that night. To top things off, when I wakened the next morning and was finishing shaving, I realized that on the wall, two inches from my head on the left side (I don't see well in the morning!) was an African wasp. He was looking like he wanted to come do his business on my forehead. Whether it's gorillas, zip lines, or wasps, these kinds of experiences push us; they make us uncomfortable.

One last example of an uncomfortable cross-cultural moment—actually much more than a moment; it was nine hours riding on an African bus from the center of Tanzania to Dar es Salaam on the Indian Ocean. I had been told that this was to be an air-conditioned bus that stopped once and showed movies. Well, the only "movies" were moving images you saw through the dirty windows on the side. There was no air conditioning except when you opened that dirty window to let the one-hundred-degree wind in. And instead of stopping once, it stopped twenty-seven times. I think the most challenging part was the way the driver managed the turns in the mountains coming down. With all the rolling and the swaying I felt I was going to meet my Redeemer at any moment.

There are lots of cross-cultural experiences which will take us out of our comfort zone, and if we undertake to do them with the right attitude, they illustrate courage. But it's not just cross-cultural experiences that reveal courage. Courage can be found in many other places. Personally, I think the bravest I had to be during my whole trip was when I spent two or three hours walking around in downtown Harare; a town that I had known and loved and lived in for two years. But as I walked there, I was reminded of the many times when my wife and my children and I had walked those same streets, and the memories that came back, that flooded me, were memories that left me sad and emotionally distraught. It required a great deal of effort to "slay those dragons" remembering all those wonderful times. It felt like I was reviewing someone else's life. So, in some ways I felt I had to be my bravest getting out of my comfort zone there in the middle of a big very familiar city.

But I saw the greatest courage in recent months as I watched my wife die. As she faced her own passing, she did so with a courage that I still find stunning and remarkable; an ability to stand up in the morning, to get up for the day and to know that it's only a matter of time. Of course, in one sense that's true for all of us, but we don't really quite know that it's so soon. Yet I saw in her, an ability to be brave, to be courageous, and to step out of her comfort zone physically, emotionally, and spiritually as well.

Finally, of course, we've seen courage in the example of Christ himself as we celebrated Christmas. Imagine the courage of leaving the infinite and squeezing yourself into the form of a baby. Imagine the courage that took. Or imagine the courage that it took for him in the Garden of Gethsemane to say to his heavenly Father, "Not my will, but thine be done" (Luke 22:42 KJV). Courage is a rare, a precious, and a powerful virtue that requires us to step out of our comfort zone.

But where does courage come from? I think in many cases, if not all cases, courage arises out of relationships. Courage arises out of love. So, we see a connection between these two virtues we've been considering today, loyalty and courage. Because love entails loyalty, and courage also arises from love, it follows that courage and loyalty are siblings and like siblings they often go together. I remember only four days before Ellen passed away, she turned to a friend and she said, "It's going to be ok because Jim said he'll give me the morphine as often as I need it." Her ability to face that situation courageously was born out of a relationship with me, and with the Lord; in short out of a confidence she had in the loyalty her Heavenly Father and I had to her.

So, what do you do with any virtue when you have it? What do you do with courage and loyalty? Well, if you remember the story about David, look at what he did when Benaniah and Abishai and Eleazar brought him water from home! He took the precious water and he *poured it out*. They had just courageously risked their lives to bring it to him, and he poured it out. David poured out the fruit of that virtue of courage. Abraham walked his "courage" up a mountain. He walked Isaac up a mountain, courageously prepared to slay his own son. And Christ, of course, in Gethsemane gave back his courage, his cross-cultural leap into this world, back to his Father and said, "Not my will, but thine be done" (Luke 22:42 KJV).

Why do people do that? Why did David pour out this gift of water, this token from home, brought by his loyal people? I think it's because he wanted God alone to satisfy his thirst. As we often sing, *"Thou and thou only, first in my heart. High king of heaven, my treasure thou art."* David's immediate thirst was not quenched that day by the acts of courage from his loyal men; but a deeper thirst was quenched that day; a deeper thirst to make it God only, *"thou and thou only."*

Last night, because I was on Africa time, I wakened at three o'clock and was awake for about an hour and a half. As I lay there thinking, my mind went to these friends of David; how did they feel about all that? Were they upset? Mind you, I think I might have been. If I had been a loyal friend to David and I had expressed that loyalty through courage to go to Bethlehem in the middle of the night, sneaking among dangerous enemies into a well, drawing water, then making it back safely to give to my friend only to see him pour it out, I might have been a little annoyed. But, I think if we're loyal and brave friends, if we act as a loyal community to one another and stretch ourselves for one another courageously, we understand that what we want for ourselves just as what we want for our friends; is that they put God first; that they put God first in their lives. I hope if you are a brave and a loyal friend today you want that, not just for yourself, but for your friends too.

So, in the end it turns out that David, not just Abishai, Eleazar, and Benaniah, but David himself was also loyal and courageous. You see, he was loyal to his Father's desire to put Him first. And he was brave to trust that relationship with his Heavenly Father enough to stay out of his comfort zone, symbolized by pouring out the taste of home that his loyal friends had brought him. He was loyal and he was courageous. And, by the way, I think we all know that Abraham got to keep Isaac. And I think we also all know, that David eventually *did* get home, to become king, not just in the stronghold, but the king in Bethlehem as well.

So today I ask you, I exhort you, as you begin a new semester; are you a loyal friend? Are you building community? Are you assuming the best?

Are you giving the benefit of the doubt? Are you comforting others? Are you nurturing your friends? That's what we want Greenville to be; a place for that. But I exhort you, too; are you brave? How brave *are* you? Are you intentionally stepping out of your comfort zone? Are you taking risks, often for others, and often out of loyalty, because you want to grow in character? Are you loyal in community? Are you brave and courageous in stepping out? But finally, and perhaps most importantly, are you sacrificially pouring out, back to him, whatever virtues God has given you? "*Thou and thou only, first in my heart. High king of heaven, my treasure thou art.*"

Let's pray.

Our Heavenly Father, we're grateful this morning for the example of heroes; for the example of mighty men and mighty women in Scripture who were loyal people, who gave their friends the benefit of the doubt; who thought the best of them. And, who, because of that relationship, out of that loyalty, were courageous. They stepped out of their comfort zones to bring relief, to bring water, to bring "a taste of home" to those they loved. Father, this morning I pray that each person in the sound of my voice would make you "first in their life." That each person within the sound of my voice would make you, the "High King of heaven," their own personal treasure for this day, for tomorrow, for next week, for the rest of this semester. As a result, Lord, may we be a community full of character that is pleasing to you and ready for service. It is in your name and to your honor that we pray these things in Jesus' name. Amen.

EPILOGUE

THE LONELIEST TRIP I EVER TOOK: HOW IT CHANGED MY LIFE... AND MAYBE YOURS TOO!

DECEMBER 2020

It has been twenty years since I delivered the earliest of the talks in this book. I published a book on philosophy of science in 1980, then one on the philosophy of education in 2000. So, I have joked that to keep up the pace, I should publish a book every twenty years, whether or not I have anything to say! At seventy years of age there will likely be no more. But I can't help but reflect on how the last twenty years have changed the world, yet *not* changed the world. Reviewing these talks, I hoped that the principles and virtues I had addressed would remain relevant and helpful even today. But I assumed that the "current events" I used to engage the hundreds of seventeen- to twenty-one-year-old students in those convocations and chapels would be terribly irrelevant. What has surprised me is that too many of the conflicts and issues illustrated in those events remain, and are if anything, more challenging now than ever.

This year, the COVID-19 virus has paralyzed our American nation, even the world. Racial tensions have flared and turned our streets into open battlegrounds for forces of social justice overlayed with those of anarchy. A presidential election has divided our people even more than in the past four years, something we didn't think possible. Friends and family, even churches have apparently lost the ability to engage in thoughtful, civil, gracious, open-minded ways. The idea of being *both* passionate in our beliefs *and* humble about them seems only a fantasy. For months, we have changed our routines, turned inward, and found ourselves anxious, facing fear, needing courage, struggling to trust, working to be disciplined, experiencing grief in new ways, yearning for grace, needing patience, and dealing with pain.

So, it turns out that not only the principles and virtues but even those current events of which I spoke those many years ago, are in a sad way still also very "current." Adding to this tragedy, many of the Christian educational institutions, like Greenville University, that have traditionally been the "points of the spear" for character education, equipping citizens of liberal democracies, have now been squeezed more and more into market driven programming that emphasizes practical career preparation and into reductions of virtue forming curricula and co-curricula. They have been strangled by government and political pressures into diluting the Christian foundations of virtue and the connections of Christian faith to these virtues.

In September of 2004 I faced a student body completely changed from the one to which I first spoke in 1999. That's the nature of academe; you have a "fresh crop" every four years. So, on the principle that good pedagogy always relies on repetition, I told them the story of a lonely trip in my life sixty years before, then closed the circle, beginning again, by repeating the analogy of our personal developmental journey to the Exodus of God's people:

> September 8, 2004
> …
> It was the loneliest trip I ever took. It changed my life and may be changing yours too! Forty-two years ago, today, I arrived in Brazil for the first time. I was barely thirteen years old, and my parents had responded to a call from the Free Methodist church for my father to serve there as President of the denominational seminary in São Paulo. We were pulled away from the tiny rural town of Spring Arbor, Michigan, away from the only friends we'd ever known, and plunked down in a city of seven million people where everyone spoke Portuguese. Despite the huge expense, my dad had asked the mission board that we be educated in an outstanding local English speaking school for children of expatriates and wealthy Brazilians, instead of sent away to boarding school for six months at a time as previous missionaries had done. So, forty-two years ago this week, I began the loneliest trip I ever took.
>
> The school was two bus rides away from our home in Tremembé da Cantareira on the north side of the city. Each bus ride was forty-five minutes long. The first one was on a public bus downtown to the busiest intersection at the heart of the city during morning rush hour. The

second was on a school bus from that intersection to the opposite outskirts of the city. The "handoff" downtown was nightmarish for a sheltered rural Michigan thirteen-year-old boy. So, my parents escorted me once, but the next day I was on my own. I remember my mother waiting with me at the public bus stop near our house. It was barely light, and it was cold! My stomach was churning so badly I thought I might throw up! She prayed with me, the bus roared to a stop, the doors hissed open, and when they hissed shut, I was entirely on my own for perhaps the first time in my life. The people were different colors, the noise was terrific, the diesel fumes made me even sicker. The odd body odors of people jammed together so closely I could hardly breathe, made me actually not want to breathe. Because of the crush, I had to stand. This meant I bent over sideways most of the trip so I could peer out the window trying desperately through the gloom to catch glimpses of the neighborhood so I could pull the rope to request a stop. I worried a lot about this. I dared not pull it too soon, but definitely not too late. The consequences of becoming lost in a city that size, not speaking a word of Portuguese, with no cell phones, and not even a phone at home...well they were unthinkable.

I remember spotting the crucial landmarks, pulling the rope, pressing almost desperately to get to the door, then landing barely on my feet on the rainy pavement of the Valley of Anhangabaú at Avenida São João; the heart of São Paulo, Brazil. The traffic was thick and noisy and smelly. My "post" was to lean against the outside of a "padaria" (bakery) and await the school bus. To this day, that mixture of smells makes me shiver with fright. While there was an approximate time of arrival, traffic made such times notoriously inaccurate. As I later came to understand, the combination of unpredictability in my arrival time and unpredictability in the arrival of the second bus made the "handoff" quasi-miraculous. I stood my post that day, leaning against an espresso bar's outside glass display case filled with Zippo cigarette lighters. I hardly dared to take my eyes from the street lest I miss the bus. It was to be an old silver bus; although in the weeks to come it sometimes wasn't a bus at all, but an oversized wooden sided station wagon called a "perúa." And I never knew which it would be. But this day it was to be the bus. The driver was a surly chain-smoking non-English speaking Japanese man who I later speculated had been a survivor at Hiroshima and hated little American boys. I knew traffic prohibited him from waiting at all, so I was convinced that my window of opportunity between hisses of the door was no more than thirty seconds or I would be stranded in downtown São Paulo for hours. But that first day I made it! And I made it most of the other days too! You can hardly imagine the relief I felt when I settled into a seat on that bus and spent the next forty-five minutes thankful that at least for the next seven hours before I began the nightmare in reverse, I had nothing more to worry about than meeting for the first time, dozens of other children that all seemed richer, smarter, and more capable than I.

On that day in 2004, speaking to that entirely new cadre of Greenville students, I began again. I repeated the ancient story of the Exodus. I pointed out that it too is the story of a trip. It is the story of a journey of "liberation." Then I urged them to consider they were embarking on a trip of their own, a liberating journey of intellectual, moral, and spiritual development. As I had for their forebears, the classes of 1999, I laid out the stages and drew the analogies I have described in Chapter One.

Then I concluded, as I do now:

I never quite got used to that lonely trip to school every day in Brazil. I guess it was one of my earliest and certainly one of my most powerful lessons in character.

It profoundly shaped my attitude toward what it means to grow inside as a person and consequently my passion for what I believe education should be. It changed my life…and so perhaps indirectly it is now changing yours. I learned that growing up is painful, stretching, and often scary. But I came to understand that by stepping out, with God beside me, in community on this liberating journey, I was capable of much much more than I ever imagined. If together today we embrace and understand that this is our calling, we will grow, and I believe the Lord will honor our efforts as our worship to Him.

So, this old man now leaves these talks with you. I hope that in a world still in turmoil, they may in some small way inspire a few to consider the path to character formation and virtue. It is rarely achieved in great measure, but is the noblest enterprise of the human condition. I believe that path is fraught with paradox, but most truly pursued by following Jesus.

INDEX

Printed in the United States
by Bookmasters